HURT NOW, LOVE LATER

HOW TO MOVE ON FROM DIVORCE

AND FIND MEANINGFUL RELATIONSHIPS

RYAN R. YOUNG

© 2018 Ryan R. Young

EMAIL: hurtnowlovelater@gmail.com
FACEBOOK: Hurt Now, Love Later
INSTAGRAM: @hurtnowlovelater

This book is dedicated to my late grandparents,

Irene and Vance McNichol.

My grandmother taught me the importance of patience, showed me the value of humor, and encouraged me never to give up on true love.

My grandfather taught me the traditional values of chivalry: treating a woman with manners and respect, and always keeping your word.

CONTENTS

Introduction... 1

Chapter 1: Achieving Acceptance 6

Chapter 2: Embracing Your Emotions................................... 17

Chapter 3: Don't Run From Your Pain................................... 33

Chapter 4: Self-Awareness 44

Chapter 5: Moving On From Your Past.................................. 59

Chapter 6: Getting Back Out There 74

Chapter 7: Building Confidence Without Arrogance 83

Chapter 8: Elevating Your Attractiveness 91

Chapter 9: Looking After Yourself.................................... 102

Chapter 10: Getting Personal 119

Chapter 11: Picking Up On The Signs................................. 128

Chapter 12: Communicating Your Qualities 137

Chapter 13: Handling The Date 149

Chapter 14: Where To Find A Potential Partner......................... 173

Chapter 15: Law Of Attraction 183

Chapter 16: Knowing It's The One.................................... 188

Chapter 17: Keeping Your Success 197

Acknowledgments... 202

INTRODUCTION

Life after ending a marriage or a long-term relationship can be an extremely difficult process, no matter how well the breakup went or the reason it happened. Whether or not there are children involved, a major breakup is never an easy thing to live with, especially if it is with someone you truly loved or, as happens in a lot of cases, are still in love with. There are many stages you will go through during this difficult time, and there are many emotions you will find yourself either enduring or trying to avoid.

As someone that has personally experienced this, I discovered it was difficult to find a book that explained just how I felt and how to deal with what I was going through. There were some that were close, but none that had everything I was looking for. That is why, years later, I have created this one. *Hurt Now, Love Later* is intended to help you understand some of the feelings you are experiencing and let you know that they are completely normal. Life may seem hopeless or intolerable now, but I promise you that it will get better. You will be happy again, quite possibly even happier than you were before the

1

breakup began. Everyone wants love, and people who say they don't have either been hurt or are running from themselves and their fears.

This book will give you an all-encompassing, first-hand look at how to deal with a major breakup and teach you the things you need to know to get over your ex and get back out there and find the love you've always wanted. We don't learn how to handle breakups or broken hearts in school, and we don't learn how to attract the person of our dreams. The whole point of this book is not only to help you understand what you're going through, but also to help you with the healing process and to gain the confidence you will need to move forward with your life and find true love, perhaps even in a much more fulfilling way than you ever thought possible.

As the author of this book, I have personally had to live through a divorce and the loss of someone I truly loved. I am giving first-hand advice that is based on personal experience and years of research and fine-tuned by considerable trial and error. Most of the books I've read have been very specific to the authors' intentions. I could find books on divorce and emotions; books on building confidence; books on communication; books on how to find a potential partner; books on how to build sexual attraction; and books on how to find and keep love. But there weren't any books that had an overall view of all these things combined. I thought to myself, "How much simpler would it be for me to learn all these things from one book?" That thought was the beginning of *Hurt Now, Love Later*.

There are so many powerful emotions and stages that accompany a divorce or a major breakup, and it's not something anyone should try to go through without help. It's important to seek help or advice, either from someone who's gone through it personally and can understand how you truly feel, or from someone who's been well educated and trained on this topic.

Simply reading about how you might be feeling or what you're going through can be a very satisfying therapeutic process. It can also help you relieve some painful emotions that have been building up inside. I know that whenever I used to read about living through a divorce, I always felt better and a little bit happier afterwards. I hope that you will feel the same relief as you read this book.

Hurt Now, Love Later is specifically designed to help you all the way through your journey, from the initial breakup to finding new love and being happy again. It will give you advice on all the beginning stages of the emotional breakup and guide you through this major transition in your life, so you will be able to truly manage your trauma and move forward with full confidence knowing that you will find love again.

Along with the research that I've included, I also share personal stories about myself and my life during the stages of my divorce, all the way through to where I am today. I hope that these glimpses into my life will help you to better see you're not the only one to go through this. Hopefully some of my stories will help raise your spirits and give you confidence that you will once again find true happiness and someone that you know you're truly in love with.

Life isn't only about the experiences we have, it's about what we do and how we handle the impacts of those experiences. Everyone who is going through divorce or a negative relationship experience has a choice when it comes to dealing with it. If you've committed to reading this book, then you've already made a choice in a positive direction. A single step in the right direction is twice as powerful as one along a negative path.

If you find this book helpful, please take a minute to post a review on Amazon. Readers' reviews (especially the ones with five stars!) make publishing on Kindle an especially gratifying experience for first-time authors like me.

Ryan Young

CHAPTER 1: ACHIEVING ACCEPTANCE

The first and probably the most difficult part of the divorce is being able to reach a state of acceptance and face the reality that your relationship has come to an end. Many people that are divorced never get to this stage because of several underlying issues. Maybe they are afraid of going through the pain and feeling of all their emotions. We will get to those a little later. Maybe they still see their ex on regular occasions because they have children together, or maybe they just haven't been able to break the attachment and familiarity that they have with their ex-partner. Perhaps it's because they just aren't ready to deal with things and may never be.

Well, don't panic. If you're reading this book, it's because you want to move on and take the next step to continue with your life. Believe me, I know what you are feeling. I've been in your shoes, maybe not exactly, but I've had to go through it, just like you will. I once was in love and bonded in marriage. When divorce came, I was stuck in resentment and sadness for a long time. I wish someone had written a book for me that I could have just read and been able to understand all the things I was feeling at the time. I needed a book where the author seemed to understand how I was feeling and could help me find relief and hope. Life isn't always easy, but it's how we manage difficult times that aim us in the direction we will take.

It's time to face the tough reality. Either you're getting divorced, or you already are divorced and want to be able to move on with your life. The sooner you learn to accept this, the sooner you will be able to understand it. You deserve to be happy, whether you made mistakes in your past relationship or not. We all deserve to be happy. (Okay, maybe not serial killers and rapists.) Facing this reality is difficult and takes courage, but it's the first and most important step in being able to move on.

Chances are that if you and/or your spouse weren't doing the right things or treating each other in the ways that you should, then you may not have been with the right person. If your ex did some things that were unimaginable to you, then you will learn to forgive them and this book will help you get there. If you committed some atrocious acts, then you will learn how to forgive yourself and regain the confidence and self-dignity that you deserve. People make mistakes. We are all human beings. There's a reason why divorce rates are so high in the world today, so understand that you are far from being alone.

The first part of being able to achieve acceptance is to understand what kind of breakup you've had. Was it through an agreement not to be together? Was there a single incident that caused a massive explosion in your relationship that was too much to recover from? Maybe it was a build-up of many, many things over a long period of time that eventually overtook both of you. Did one person meet someone else, or suddenly fall out of love with the other? Or even, the worst possible thought, maybe you're no longer together because of death.

Death can be devastatingly traumatic, and we've all experienced it in one way or another at some points during our lives. It's a completely different matter when it happens to your partner or someone you are in love with. It's painful even to imagine that kind of event happening to us. Oddly enough, though, the point could be made that dealing with a divorce or breakup that doesn't involve death can be even more difficult than having a spouse pass away.

The reasoning behind this is that when someone passes away, it is completely out of our hands. There is no going back and it is irreversible. When the other person is still living, however, you might think that there is a chance you can rekindle things. Or maybe you still need to see that person occasionally, and that makes it difficult to move on. Worse yet, maybe you even must see them with another partner. No matter what your situation is, you will learn to move on from it, regardless of how hard it's been.

Another factor that I should bring up at this point is time. This is something many people will probably tell you is important, and unfortunately it is. Time is one of those things that we all want more of and don't want to waste, but if we try moving on too quickly and ignore what's happening inside of us, we could just end up slowing ourselves down in the end. A lot of people say that it takes half the time that you were in a relationship with someone to get over them. So, if you were with someone for ten years, then it would take five years to truly get over them.

I don't really believe in this being a precise formula, as I think each case is unique and maybe someone's relationship was on death row for years already and nobody had the courage to end it. In my eyes, the sooner you can accept that your relationship is over, the sooner you will be able to start the healing process, and the sooner you will be able to move on and find love again.

People aren't shown how to deal with love or broken hearts in school. Unfortunately, you need to find specific books online or in the self-help aisle of a book store. We literally need to source our own solutions to the problem and try to fix it ourselves (a.k.a. self-help). Sometimes I used to joke around about being able to put a couple of bandages on my heart and get back out there. The funny thing is, that's kind of true to an extent. Well, without using bandages.

You see, your heart truly has been broken or ruptured in some way or another and it needs to be mended before you can properly move on. But just like anything else on your body, it needs time to heal. Once you've accepted what's happened to you and the reality sets in, you will be able to apply the necessary bandages. With some time, your body will heal itself, but it's going to need your help if it's going to heal properly. The good news is that you want to heal yourself and you've moved in the right direction. Just like having a bad wound, you need to go to a doctor or seek help to get stitched up and bandaged, and then through time and the proper treatment, your wound will be gone.

One thing that you will eventually begin to understand is that you don't necessarily have to be over what happened. It's more about being over the person that it happened with. Life goes on, and you will meet someone new that you will create new memories with. Even if you don't meet someone new or you just become so picky that it takes a long time to find the prime candidate, you will still create new memories on your own that will ease the blow of the old ones.

I truly believe that everyone who enters our lives does so because they are meant to. We are all meant to graze each other's paths in one way or another, and we are meant to take experiences from each other that will impact us as individuals. Take what you can from that person and the experiences they gave you. Use them to grow stronger and wiser. I was extremely hurt from my ex-partner in many ways, yet I learned many things from my experiences with her, whether they were good or bad. I've been able to find a place in my life where I have true happiness, which I wouldn't have had if I had remained in a relationship with her.

My new partner often wonders how I can look back and not have extreme and hateful resentment towards my ex, but I am so much further than that. It's not until you are able to look back and be able to realize that they were not right for you and that there's no need for resentment and that you still want happiness for that person, that you truly know you have gotten over them. If you still have anger towards them, it's usually a clear indication that you have more work to do. We will discuss more about this in an upcoming chapter about emotions.

Shame can also play a factor in not being able to accept what has happened, especially when there is family involved. For me, this part was a tough obstacle; at least, I thought it was going to be a lot tougher than it was. This also cost me some time when I should have addressed it earlier. A lot of people will try to stay together for the kids or because the families are deeply connected with yourself or your partner. Personally, I was extremely close with my ex-wife's side, mostly with my brother-in-law. I was always afraid of letting him down or him not being a part of my official family anymore. We were essentially best friends in many ways.

Another person I was deathly afraid of letting down was my father. While I was growing up, my father was a man of few words who spoke only when he had thoroughly thought out what he was going to say before the words left his lips. He has always been a good man and always looked after me the way a father should, but it wasn't until I got a bit older that we grew as close as we are today. Other than being a hard worker and always being a motivated guy, I probably didn't do all that much growing up that I thought would make him proud of me. I mean, I was never a bad kid. I stayed off drugs, did well at work, respected my parents, but there was nothing too far off the grid for him to be especially proud of me - until my wedding day.

It was a perfect day. It was everything I could have imagined it to be, and at the time I was very deeply in love. Everyone was dancing and having a great time when my father ushered me outside to view the perfect evening from an outside perspective. As we stood there, outside the window looking in, it was as if time had stopped altogether. We talked about what a great night it had been, and my father's warm arm wrapped around my shoulder and pulled me in snugly. He looked at me with quivery, watery eyes and told me how he couldn't be prouder of the man I had become.

As you can imagine it would be extremely tough, years later, to tell my father he no longer had a reason to be proud of me. At least, that was how I viewed it at the time. The thing is, though, you will find that people are a lot more understanding than you think, especcially the people who truly care for you. As a matter of fact, when I finally told my parents, they were so understanding that it drew my father and me even closer to one another than before.

If you fear moving forward, then you will always be stuck in your past. It's okay to feel fear when you understand it and embrace it. It's okay to fear the future and what people will think. Accept that fear is part of the package and that you must still move forward. Your family will show you the same love and respect that you show them. If you do not have a good relationship with them, then perhaps those are future relationships you can work on.

Your friends will also be there for you. Some may have already seen it coming. You will need their support so you can rely on them to talk to or seek advice. You see, even if you had a bad relationship, you will have to get used to your partner not being in your life in the same way that they always were. Even if your partner didn't listen to you, they were still that person you could come home to and talk to about your day or tell your problems to or share your excitement with. When that person has been there for years and is suddenly gone, you will need to lean on friends and family members around you.

I have a piece of artwork in my home that represents a time in my life when I was going through my divorce and it says, "When it hurts to look back and you're afraid to look ahead, look beside you and there will be your friends." This saying has really stuck with me, and the words emphasize how important the relationships around me are. Think about it. Wouldn't you be there for the ones that you love in their times of need? Hell, I'm betting they'd love to find any excuse to sit down over a beer or glass of wine. Trust me, use this support as much as you can. It will make you feel great just talking to the people around you and letting it vent out. It's an important part of the healing process.

Telling your friends also means you are starting to "accept it." If you've lost or let go of some of your friendships, then now's the time to rebuild them. A friend of mine who knew what I had been through with my divorce called me out of nowhere after I hadn't spoken with him in over three years. He explained to me that he was experiencing a similar thing. He needed someone who had been there. He needed my support and advice. He needed my friendship.

Since then, this person and I have become best friends, and still to this day, even though we are both in new relationships, we make time to spend together. Sometimes we hang out without our new partners and sometimes as couples. Regardless, we won't lose touch again like we did in the past. We value our friendship too much and we learned from our past mistakes why it's so important to keep the right friendships in your life. Keeping up with your friendships also plays a key role in your personal happiness and will have positive impacts on your relationships with a partner.

CHAPTER 2: EMBRACING YOUR EMOTIONS

Emotions play a key part in being able to be happy with your life again. Just like an overbearing mother-in-law, they will come and go as they please, and if you don't come to terms with them, they will take you over and be out of control. You don't have to deal with them every time they pop up, but at the very least you do need to acknowledge that they are there and handle them later. Emotions can get quite complicated, and you can break them down and analyze them to considerable depth, but I will keep my explanations as clear and straightforward as I can.

I have read numerous books on research that involve the basic emotions that you will feel during a breakup. There are several feelings that you will be experiencing, but the four main ones you need to acknowledge are fear, sorrow, sadness, and anger. You may feel one more than others, but at some point, you will have to face them all.

The goal is that you will need to deal evenly with each emotion. These four emotions play as opposites to one another. What I mean by this is that your sadness plays opposite to your anger and your fear opposite to your sorrow. You will find it difficult to relieve one without the other, and without feeling them all, you will never truly get over your traumatic experience with your ex-partner. You may be able to move on and find someone else, but, believe me, you will find it difficult to be truly happy with your new life if you've swept your dirty emotions under the rug.

Your new partner will eventually be looking around your house one day and find what you've hidden. So, let's all man (or woman) up and take care of them. Women are a little (sometimes a lot) more in touch with their emotions, so, fellas, we may have some extra work to do here, but the rewards will be worth all of it.

Now, with all the dating sites and ways of meeting people today you may be tempted to get out there and start trying your luck before you're ready. I will talk about the best ways and some of the better sites I've found to be successful, but for now, don't go out there breaking too many hearts. That's not to say you can't venture out and meet friends or people to have casual sex with as long as you're being honest with the people you are doing things with. This book will help you develop and portray certain traits to attract the person you are looking for, but that's all still to come. For now, let's continue with the healing.

ANGER AND SADNESS

Anger and sadness are generally the stronger and more dramatic of the four emotions. As thoughts flow through your mind, the corresponding emotions will come along with them. Anger and sadness are usually the first ones that surface after a major breakup. Perhaps you are feeling angry about something that your partner did. You may be thinking "How could they do this to me?" or "Don't they love me?" or maybe "I hate them for doing this!"

Perhaps it's yourself that you're angry with, and you're saying "I'm so mad at myself!" and "How could I do this?" Whether it's you or your partner that you're targeting, they are still all feelings of anger. This is normal and it's okay to feel this. You need to feel this. If the timing is right and you're alone, then try to embrace it and feel the anger. Even try yelling out loud or screaming. This is good for you to do, especially in the beginning. Just like sadness, anger is a powerful emotion and unhealthy to hold in for too long.

If you plan to get loud, go for a walk or a drive somewhere that you can be alone, somewhere you can let yourself go completely. Find a safe place where you don't have to worry about being heard. Of course, you don't want to end up somewhere you might get lost. If that's a possibility, make sure you let someone know where you're going.

Chances are that sadness will follow directly after. Anytime I dealt with anger I found that sadness was waiting behind it and ready to pounce on me. As I said, they are opposites of each other, so it only makes sense that sadness would follow anger or vice versa. Sadness may come with questions such as "Why would you do this?" or "What's the family going to think?" or maybe "Why doesn't he or she care?"

It's just as important to feel sadness as it is anger. Men tend to shy away from sadness because they think it makes them look weak, but feeling sad is important and you will become stronger in the end for it. Besides, women find it very attractive when a man can be in touch with his feelings. It shows that he has the capability to show sympathy for others and therefore has a good "mating quality." Out of all the emotions, sadness was probably the one I was most stuck in. I was just plain sad that I had invested so much of myself into something that didn't work out.

Even though it's important to feel sadness, be careful that it is genuine sadness and that you aren't just feeling sorry for yourself. These are two completely different things. Don't beat yourself up and pity yourself for what's happened. Feel sadness for the situation and what happened, but don't feel sorry for yourself. This situation you're in is only temporary, and the sooner you accept the feelings you need to feel, the sooner you will be in a much better place.

Whether it's mainly you or your ex-partner that you feel angry and sad towards, chances are that you will have at least some of these feelings about both of you. There's usually reasons on both sides for why things worked out the way that they did, and it's important to feel the anger and sadness that you may be feeling about both of you. Whether you blame yourself, your ex, or both of you, the blame will eventually diminish and you will come to terms with what happened and be able to concentrate on just the emotions themselves.

FEAR AND SORROW

These two emotions tend to surface more so when a bit of the anger and sadness has been addressed already. They may come across as being less powerful than the other two emotions, but don't be fooled. They are still just as formidable and play a crucial role in the healing process. Fear is the type of emotion that will concern you with issues in the future. There might be thoughts like "What if I never find love again?" or "What if I'm going to be alone forever?" or maybe "Our family will never be the same."

Fear may cause you anxiety at times when you think about it and feel it, but try to relax and embrace it. It's completely normal, and you need to feel this emotion. Again, remember that many people have been in this same situation, including me, and later, when we discuss ways of gaining self-confidence, I will help you with this and any fear of what lies ahead. Just concentrate on the emotion of fear itself for now and know why you feel this way. Think about what it is that you're afraid of and don't shy away from the fear. The more that you can understand its presence, the more easily you will conquer it.

We all experience fear in life and it's a large contributor to why many people never get to enjoy the things they should in their lifetime. Fear can prevent your happiness. You need to get over your fear, and the only way to do that is to address them and understand them. It's okay to be afraid, but it's not okay to let fear run your life. It will come up several more times in your life and the more you get to know it, the more you will recognize it and acquire the ability to overcome it.

Sorrow is almost a form of sadness, but relates to more of what could have happened with your past partner, but didn't. Feeling sorrow was one of the tougher emotions to bring up for me because it wasn't something I felt quite as easily as the others. Sorrow didn't just come out on its own. and perhaps it was because I was still experiencing some denial of what had happened and I hadn't truly reached acceptance yet.

Therefore, being able to accept the breakup is such an important first step. Sorrow may bring about thoughts like "We never had the child we wanted," or "We didn't ever go to Paris as we'd planned," or, if you were common law, maybe "we didn't even get married as we wanted." I found that when I brought up sorrow, it would almost cycle me right back into sadness or anger. This is okay to do, but you should try to genuinely feel the sorrow and not just let it go or move it to the back of your memory bank or sweep it under the rug, as I discussed earlier. Again, these emotions are equally important, not only bring up, but to feel, which leads me to my next point.

Now that you know what the important emotions to recognize are, it's time to know about why they are important and how to deal with them properly. There has been a lot of research on these emotions, none of which I have scientifically collected myself, but I have learned from the people that have done the ground work and I'm able to pass it on it you. That's the great part about living in the current era. So much research has already been done, and we can educate ourselves from so many sources and implement findings from the perspective of multiple individuals and give ourselves the best all-encompassing and "informed" solution.

GETTING STUCK

This next part that I'm about to tell you is very important, and I encourage you to pay especially close attention. "If you do not feel each emotion equally, <u>you can get stuck in a single emotion</u>." What I mean by this is, for example, if you are feeling sadness all the time, you can get stuck in being sad and find it difficult to get out. Just giving yourself time will not be enough. Remember what I said earlier about these emotions being opposites of each other? Well, that is why it's important. If you are constantly feeling sadness and can't get out, it's because you need to equally feel anger equally. The same goes for feeling angry all the time.

You need to address and feel your sadness equally. You may be thinking "Well, I'm not sad. I'm so angry because of how they treated me." Trust me, there is an underlying sadness there. The same goes for feeling fear all the time; it's because you need to equally feel the sorrow. These emotions all play a complex role with one another and none of them are more important than the other.

For myself, I tended to be stuck in sadness all the time. I had so much to be angry about, but I just couldn't get away from the absolute and powerful emotion of sadness. The beginning of the breakup tends to be the most abrupt and therefore can be difficult to cope with. When you're used to going to bed and waking up with your partner right next to you and suddenly that person just isn't there anymore, it can be very difficult and just plain sad!

This was exactly the case for me. My ex and I were quite active together, and we were like best friends, spending every weekend and doing the things we both enjoyed together. After the breakup, I tried to continue to do these things to ease my pain and stay busy, but it seemed to be more difficult because she wasn't there anymore, and I still I had the familiarity of being with her.

It wasn't until I found myself stuck in sadness for quite some time that I knew I needed to do something about it. I just couldn't take it anymore. That's when I started my adventure of finding and learning as much information as I possibly could. I began reading as many books as possible, pursuing the aid of a counselor, and getting involved with groups of people that were going through the same things or had already been through them. I also researched as much as I could online and wherever else I could find vital information.

Eventually I found the answers that I needed to be able to understand why these emotions are essential to becoming happy and breaking the "familiarity" that you had with your ex-partner. Being able to feel the anger along with the sadness was the answer for me to get away from being stuck in the same place for so long. It's okay to feel the sadness, but I needed to equally feel the anger. My counselor at the time taught me to address the sadness by saying "I feel sad, but I'm going to put it aside for now and come back to it a bit later." That enabled me not to ignore how I was feeling, but to address it and at the same time to put it aside so that I could move on from it and come back to it later.

Then it was time for me to bring up the anger. I had to try to think of what made me mad. Whether it was a particular event, or how I was treated, or the fact that I felt betrayed and left behind, I found that the anger was easier to get to than I thought. Before I knew it, I was in an isolated area screaming at the top of my lungs and shaking my fists in the air like an angry gorilla. I may or may not have even done this in public a few times too!

When you take the time to address that you have an emotion, you might find that you have more of that emotion than you expected. Take the time to feel that emotion and go through it. Don't ignore it and sweep it under the rug. Face it head-on and take the time to feel it. Your body has these emotions for a reason. Keep bringing these emotions up when you can, and do that repeatedly until they become less and less. Take the time to address these emotions and feel them equally, and eventually you will get to a place of relief and contentment where you will start to see the light in your future and the possibility of moving on and finding love and happiness again, as you deserve!

STAYING COMMITTED TO THE BREAKUP

During the emotional healing process, it can be easy to stray from what you are going through and have hopes that maybe somehow this is temporary and things may work out. It's important to stay committed to the breakup during the healing process. It will be difficult to truly get over things if, in the back of your head, you're thinking that your ex-partner will have a complete change of heart and come running back to you. This will hold you back from believing in getting over things and lead you into not accepting what has happened. So stay committed to the breakup.

I'm guilty of not staying committed to the breakup with my ex-wife, and all that did was prolong the healing process for myself. I tried getting over things, but I wasn't truly believing that what I was doing was permanent. All I really achieved was to completely waste my own time and make myself feel desperate. Those are not good feelings to have, and you are going through enough negative feelings anyway, so don't add more to your plate and your stress levels. The more you can control the number of negative emotions you are feeling, the easier it will be to get over the ones you already have and create new positive emotions in place of the negative ones.

ACCEPTING THAT YOU HAVE NO CONTROL OVER OUTCOMES

It's not easy to accept that you have no control over outcomes. I think everyone tends to think if they had just done something differently or had changed slightly. then the outcome would have been different or they could have saved the relationship. Don't carry this monkey on your back. The outcome is what it is, and you couldn't have done anything differently. If you broke up due to an addiction problem, for instance, then you may have been able to change it during the relationship, but you still need to accept that you didn't change and the outcome still can't be changed.

You may also think you may be able to win their heart if you just slightly change how you dress or make them jealous so you can seduce them and overwhelm them with the irresistibility of you. Maybe if you play it cool and try to get their attention by making yourself desirable, they won't be able to move on and will come running back and willing to change everything and start fresh. I will tell you now, none of that stuff will work. That's just not accepting what's happened and not committing to the breakup. You will make yourself look desperate and even less attractive.

You need to accept that you can't control the outcome and you can't control other people's feelings. You need to let the situation play out freely while dealing with your own issues and not try to control the situation and other people's feelings. Your situation is the only situation that you truly have control over.

COMPARING YOURSELF TO OTHERS

So, let's say you're walking around the mall doing a little bit of shopping, and everywhere you look, you see happy couples all around you. Everyone else's life just seems so perfect and it feels like you're the only one that doesn't have the love of their life wrapped around their arm. This is a prime example of comparing your life to another people's lives. Other people's lives are not as perfect as they seem. Two people could be in a perfect relationship today, and, in a couple of weeks, one of them could be in a traumatic accident and change their lives forever. Remember that your current situation is temporary and only for now.

You also need remember that you're only noticing other couples more because that's what you're concentrating on and that's what is a big part of your life now. Have you ever bought a new car and then, as soon as you're driving it around, you start noticing the same car everywhere? It's only because you're concentrating on it and it's a part of your life that you notice that it seems like everyone else has the same car. Or maybe you started working for a new company and you start seeing their vehicles driving around everywhere. It's the same thing. So don't worry if you feel like everyone else seems happy, and stop comparing your own situation to theirs.

This is also the case with looking at other people's social media. People only show their lives in a positive way and don't advertise the crappy parts of their life. If you're comparing your "downs" to their "ups," then you're not comparing apples to apples. They could be going through difficult times that you are unaware of, so it isn't fair of you to compare your real life to their social media life. Don't dwell on it, and don't feel sorry for yourself. Take the positive in your life, be thankful for what you have, and grow from it. Stop beating yourself up. Everyone has the power to create the life that they deserve.

CHAPTER 3: DON'T RUN FROM YOUR PAIN

Running from something that hurts us is an instinct that's built into us from the time of birth. It's quite simple, really: if it hurts, then move away from it or stop doing whatever it is that's causing you pain. For example, if you hold your hand over a candle, it's going to really hurt and you will pull your hand away. If you touch something sharp, it's going to cut you, so you learn not to touch it, because again it hurts.

Let's analyze this a bit more. Just because a candle burns us when it's lit, that doesn't mean that we can't touch it again. We just need to know not to touch it when there's a flame. And just because we touch something sharp and it cuts us, that doesn't mean that we can't learn to touch it properly. Maybe it's a knife, and we need to learn how to touch the handle or another part of the knife that won't injure us. The same goes with running from your feelings because they are painful, instead of learning how to deal with them properly.

It's so easy to feel hurt and just bury your feelings for now and deal with them later. I know this, because I did it for quite some time. I just didn't want to face my realities and it was much easier for me to go out with my friends and get drunk. I wasn't ever an alcoholic, at least not in my eyes, but it could be that I was using alcohol as a tool to forget my pain or hide from it. I was never a person to come home from work and have a drink, and I will never be that person, but I more than made up for it on the weekends.

I also used to bury myself in work so deeply that I forgot my personal life for a while. This did wonders for my career, but it sure didn't do a damned thing for my life outside of work. You may go through a period where you just aren't ready to deal with it yet and that's okay. In fact, I almost think it's a necessary step to go through this part. It's better to be that way now than it is to get back into a relationship and then need to go through it afterwards, when you're already involved.

Most likely you would just bounce from relationship to relationship without any true commitment, or you might possibly just sacrifice your own happiness and just settle down for the sake of it. You don't want to be that person, so allow yourself to go through this transition before you start looking for the right person to spend the rest of your life with.

If you are going to run out there and terrorize the town as the newly-single opportunist that wants to make up for lost time, be aware of this and use it only as a temporary relief and not a permanent lifestyle. I will show you ways of being able to attract others and create an "aura" about yourself that will make you somewhat irresistible to your preferred sex, but it can get carried away and become too much of a temporary relief, and you will end up with self-hate and unhappiness.

Again, I know this from personal experience that I will share with you throughout this book. There comes a time when you need to take a stand and face the reality. There comes a time where you will need to take responsibility for your part of your failed relationship, and own it. Of course, if your breakup was from death, then obviously, this would be different. If it was from death you may still have some things in the relationship to take ownership for to help you along with the healing process.

I, myself, got caught up in the temporary relief of meeting other people and having short-term relationships with them. The more I did it, the better I got at it. I researched several methods of being able to attract my opposite sex, and then I acted on them. I tried them all, having both successes and failures. I learned what to do and how to do it and even when to do it. Through my failures, I learned what worked and what didn't. I learned how to attract people online and, even more so, in person.

But this was not the lifestyle that I desired, and I truly became unhappy. I hated my life at that time and I didn't like myself or where I was going. My family and friends all knew that I had the ability to meet people and have them desire me, but they also felt sad knowing that I wasn't truly happy. Of course, my friends loved living vicariously through me and used to constantly try to press me for stories. You might be thinking "What guy wouldn't love to have vicarious sex with multiple beautiful women?" I became very good at attracting the opposite sex and had just the right amount of self-confidence and other traits that made me desirable to potential partners. I was a trained, silver tongued, suave, successful and poised man. I will cover some of this in the chapter "Building Confidence without Arrogance."

During that time, I often felt emotions like guilt and remorse. I think this is a normal reaction when living that type of lifestyle. How could I be proud of myself or like myself when I was just running from what was really bugging me? I knew that what I really wanted was to be in love again, and I knew that I had work to do on myself before I could go down that road again. Unfortunately, I had to virtually hit rock bottom before facing the realities of what I needed to do in my life.

I was never one to drive slowly and that night was no different. I was speeding on a night where the roads were wet, and, to make things worse, I wasn't driving the sports car that I owned at the time. Instead, I was driving the brand-new truck that my employer had just bought for me. Besides my not being used to how the vehicle performed, the truck was also a two-wheel drive, making it light in the back end, and it had a very large 6.2-litre engine in the front.

I had a lot going on in my mind that night and I was traveling at a high speed, knowing that I had a friend waiting at my house for me. I approached an "S" curve, and the back end of the truck kicked out on me and fishtailed. I tried to recover, but it was too late and I was going too fast. The truck shot off the road and over the sidewalk, where I collided with the back end of a parked 18-wheel semi-truck trailer. The impact was so hard that it literally peeled the whole front of the truck apart like a can opener. The driver-side quarter panel flew off the truck and came through the windshield, stopping right in front of my face with barely what was left of an airbag between us.

The truck was demolished. All four tires were flat, and one of them was detached from the vehicle. The crumple zones took everything they could, and eventually the cab of the truck began to crush. The windshield and side windows shattered. It was a total wreck.

I was lucky enough to walk away from the vehicle completely unharmed other than a few bruises, minor scratches and some glass stuck in my legs. This happened the night before my mother's birthday. My family and I all went to view the site of the accident another day, and we were also able to see what was left of the vehicle. Seeing that crumpled mess brought tears to my family's eyes, including my own. I just couldn't believe what I had walked away from. It seemed impossible for anyone to survive such wreckage.

I never want to put myself or my family through that again. I knew right then and there that I had been put on this planet for a reason and that I had to make some major changes in my life. I didn't want to die without the fulfilled life that I was supposed to be living or make my parents deal with losing me. I also didn't want to hurt someone else. It was time to act on the next chapter of my life, one where I learned to love myself and be truly happy with the life that I was living. It was time to be a man and face my realities. It was time to stop running from my pain.

Sometimes when people are in a relationship, they can become reliant on the other person or on the relationship itself to give them happiness. This is something a lot of people do. Then, when the relationship ends, their happiness is immediately gone and it can feel like their whole world is crashing down. Therefore, it is imperative when you enter a relationship where you and your partner are happy with yourselves as individuals.

It's really about sharing your lives and happiness together, and that makes it easier to let both people be free within the relationship. While you are facing your realities and your feelings, it's still important to enjoy your current life. Do the things that you enjoy and spend time with your friends. This will help you create happiness at the same time.

MEDITATION

Another thing I would highly recommend is meditation. Don't laugh! It can work wonders for your happiness and stress levels. I was skeptical of this at first, but meditation is simply a way of relaxing and letting go of things. You literally just sit there and think of nothing. It's harder than you think! Try it sometime.

Before bed, take an extra ten minutes and sit down in a quiet place without distraction. Close your eyes and concentrate on your breathing. As thoughts enter your mind, try to dismiss them immediately. Our minds tend to have thoughts constantly entering them. It's that little voice in the back of your head that's always talking to you and telling you stories or judging everything around you, including yourself. Every time a thought enters your mind, let it flow right out, and just think of nothing. It sounds simple, but once you try it you will see just how difficult it can be.

Try it for ten minutes a night, and, as you get a bit better at it, try to work your way up to twenty minutes. The more you do it, the better you will feel. When you have a lot of mental stress and feelings that you're dealing with, it's important to rest your mind and keep it fresh. This will also help you sleep better at night as you become relaxed before hitting the sack. You might even find yourself smiling while you are doing it. You can even start to add some peaceful music in the background at the same time. It may seem foreign to you, but try something new. After all this whole book revolves around creating a change in your life, so give it an honest try and I promise you the results will be positive for you.

WRITING A LETTER

One key activity I tried to relieve some pain was to write a letter to my ex. I got this idea from one of my counselors and found it to work quite well. The trick, though, is that you will never give the letter to your ex. Because they will never see it or read it, you can write whatever you like . Include anything and everything you want to tell them: all your anger, sadness, the things you won't get to do with them, why you aren't together anymore…everything!

I wrote mine over several days. Whenever I started having a powerful emotion come up or I had thoughts of my ex-partner pop into my head, I would start writing about how I was feeling towards her.

Although you consciously know that your ex will never see what you're writing to them, take the time to write the letter as if they were really going to receive it. Pretend that this is the very last communication that you will ever have with them, and don't hold back. This also helps you with embracing your emotions and getting them out.

Once you have taken the time to write down all your emotions, you don't have to do anything with the letter at that point. You may decide to hold onto it for a while and that's just fine. You may even want to add things to it here and there over a period of time. I kept my letter for quite a while before I was finally ready for the next step. You can also write only a little bit at a time. You can take as long as you want, and don't need to feel the need to be pressured to get it done. If you're having a bad day and your emotions are getting to you, try picking up the letter and writing some more.

This next step may seem as odd to you as it did to me. When you get to the point where you feel like you've written all that you want to say, then the letter is complete. When you're ready and have some time to yourself when you can go somewhere quiet, take the letter and go there. You may have already read the letter back to yourself while writing it, but this will be the very last time you read it. When you're reading it pretend that you are reading it to your ex and that they are sitting right there in front of you. You may feel a lot of emotions passing through you as you go through this exercise, and that is a good thing to have happen.

Now here comes the odd part. Once you've completed reading the letter, burn it. That's right! Now of course you are going to want to do this in a safe environment where you won't start anything else on fire or hurt yourself, so I recommend doing this in an actual fire pit. I was fortunate enough that I found a picnic area with a proper fire pit where I could place it and let it burn. I also made sure to bring a bottle of water with me to be certain that the letter was extinguished after it had finished burning.

Now, it may seem like an extreme step to burn the letter, but it's a great way to release your emotions and feel that you've finally told them just how you feel. It can make you feel like you've physically gotten rid of your emotions that have been pent up inside you. You don't even need to burn it. Just writing it out and reading it as if your ex was there is a helpful step, but if you're comfortable burning it, that will take the release of your emotions one step further.

CHAPTER 4: SELF-AWARENESS

If you aren't familiar with the term "emotional intelligence" I highly recommend learning a bit about it at some point. It might help you in more ways than you can imagine with your personal relationships and your business relationships. The reason I bring up emotional intelligence is because it revolves around not only being self-aware, but also being aware of your surroundings and the people around you.

I have read several books on this topic, as well as taking several courses around the country to better develop my self-awareness and improve my emotional intelligence. I believe knowing about emotional intelligence can help you to better understand yourself and how you are feeling. It can also help you when you are eventually ready to meet new people and have new relationships.

I can go into great depth and detail about all the different types of personalities out there and how to recognize them, classify them, and adjust yourself accordingly, but I'm going to keep this fairly basic for now. There is so much information and training available on this topic that I might even be able to write an entire book on just that one subject, but that's way more than we need to get into right now.

This is how your EQ (emotional quotient) works. Similar to your IQ (Intelligent Quotient) there are a variety of tests you can take in person or online that will give you an exact score of your EQ level. The major difference between IQ and EQ, though, is that your IQ never really changes throughout your life. It just is what it is. The good part about EQ is that you can develop it and improve it over time. The more you work on your self-awareness, the more self-aware you will become and the higher your EQ score will be.

Another awesome fact about emotional intelligence is that many of the successful and wealthy entrepreneurs of the world today don't necessarily have high IQ's, but their EQ's are usually through the roof. This is because they have been able to train themselves to be aware of themselves and build their professional relationships to be the best they can be. The same goes for their personal relationships.

Being self-aware means that you understand the emotion that you are feeling at a given time and are able to own that feeling. When you are feeling angry, first admit to yourself that you are feeling angry.

Secondly, ask yourself "Why am I feeling angry right now?" There's usually a simple solution to this. Maybe someone is saying something to upset you, or someone isn't listening to you.

The best way to handle this is not to get angry because it won't help you or the situation, especially if you're dealing with someone who has an "A" type personality. This type of personality is very driven, demanding, and can be stubborn and unwilling to hear what you need to say. They tend to have the "my way or the highway" type of mentality, unless they have trained themselves to be self-aware and have a higher EQ. Then they would be willing to work with you.

Once you have figured out what's annoying you, it will become easier for you to control that emotion. It takes practice and patience to improve and hone these skills, but with time and being constantly aware of your emotions, they will get better. You will find yourself being less reactive and making more informed decisions, rather than letting your emotions decide for you. This is going to be a major asset for you in life when entering new relationships, no matter what the type of relationship. If this is something that interests you, I suggest looking up the topic of emotional intelligence training online or picking up a book at your local bookstore or library.

Whenever I meet someone new, I can usually tell what type of personality they have within seconds. I'm sure most of you know what I mean and do the same thing, even if it's sub-consciously. You can always tell the difference between someone who is assertive and someone who is quiet and more passive. If you treat them with the same type of personality in return, it won't aid in your communication with them very well.

If you are assertive with another assertive person, both of you will be constantly trying to overpower one another and will struggle to get anywhere in the conversation. If you are very passive and shy with another person that is passive and shy, there won't be much of a conversation at all. That's not to say that you should become very assertive with a shy person, because they won't react to that very well either. You need to treat them with respect and ask them questions and get them to come out of their shells a bit. Maybe you could make them laugh and feel comfortable around you so that they begin to feel like they can communicate with you.

One of the courses that I have taken for work was on negotiation skills and how to strengthen relationships. A really helpful thing I learned from that course was that it usually isn't the person who does all the talking that controls the conversation, but it's more so the person doing the listening and asking the questions.

Hopefully, by now, it is clear why I have included a chapter about self-awareness in this book. Being upset with your breakup and having spurts of emotions throughout your day can cause mood swings. As a result, you may be a little more reactive with the people around you and possibly tarnish relationships at work and with people that are close to you. Self-awareness will also help you understand what part of the healing process you are in. We tend to always think we are further ahead than we are with healing, but remember that the brain heals faster than the heart.

Your brain may get to a point where it's telling you, "All right, it's been long enough and it's time to move on, you sissy!" And that's exactly what you might try to do, but eventually you will get to a point where your heart catches up with you and you won't be ready to move on properly or it will hold you back. The process of healing is more about feelings than it is about thoughts, so unfortunately you can't ignore your heart and move on before it's ready to.

This is also why I kept finding myself having short-term relationships that wouldn't last longer than a couple of months. I would feel great in the beginning, and then out of nowhere I would feel trapped or even lose my attraction to that person all together. I would then move on and find the next person and repeat the process to feel that temporary relief of pain, and so on and so on, until it turned into a vicious cycle.

That's not to say that I didn't enjoy being with those people. Most of them were fantastic individuals, but I just wasn't ready and it wasn't meant to be. I would catch myself finding the smallest things I didn't like about them, and I would use those characteristics as excuses for myself not to like them or to get out of the relationship.

BE HONEST WITH YOURSELF Take the time to really listen to yourself, and I don't mean listen to your head. Listen to your gut feelings, and don't ignore them. You're going to go through several stages when you've had a major breakup, and being honest with yourself isn't as easy as it seems. Remember, a serious breakup can be quite traumatic to your body.

Much like a car accident, your body suffers from a type of trauma or shock that causes damage to your emotional and psychological well-being. If you've had a major car accident you can't just expect to get out of that car and jump into the next one and drive off as if nothing happened. You may have to go through treatments like rehabilitation, physiotherapy, and massage therapy. The same principles apply with a traumatic breakup. You can't expect to jump into the next relationship without going through some form of rehabilitation.

There's just no skipping this part, as much as I would prefer to tell you that there is. You need to be honest with yourself and give yourself the time that is needed to heal, helping it along the way with some form of rehabilitation. I'm not saying you need to see any kind of professional doctor, but use the resources around you to help yourself. Counseling can help. I wouldn't say it's an absolute must, although I did find some benefits to it, but I would still recommend it. Counseling helped me by allowing me to talk to someone without having to hold back or worry about what I was saying or the information that I was sharing. Being able to talk enabled me to bring up my emotions and accelerate the healing process.

Also, read books like this one. There are lots of self-help books out there, and reading them was a great way for me to get an all-round support and perspective on things. Try to be aware of how you are feeling and act upon it. Sometimes, going to my local bookstore and just starting to read made me feel good because I was reading about people that knew what I was going through. I always left the bookstore feeling better than when I walked in. It seemed to be quite healing for me, and it was a lot better than just going out and having a drink with my buddies. It made me feel like I was making progress. and during such a harsh time for me, that was the encouragement that I needed.

BE HONEST WITH OTHERS If you're going to see other people during your healing process, then tell them what you're experiencing. Tell them you're going through a divorce or that you've just had a major breakup. Don't be afraid to be honest with them, and they will be understanding about your situation. I'm not saying that's the first thing you need to tell them, but if you plan to have any kind of relationship with them, you should tell them your circumstances. You don't have to go into any kind of detail about why or what happened, but just give them the courtesy of providing the basics.

This was one thing I always did, and I don't regret. If that person decides they don't want to get involved with you because of it, then that's their right. You can't decide that for them, and you will have to let them make their own decision. Most of the time, you will find that they will still want to move forward with you, and if they don't then, you should let them move on. You may even find that down the road that person changes their mind or comes to you after you've done some healing, but for now it's important that you accept and respect their decision.

Put it this way: if you end up pursuing a relationship with them now, before you've completed your healing process, it's possible that things may not work out for you and there may be some type of bridge burned along the way. If you don't enter a relationship with them until after you've completed your healing process, it's more likely that you will be successful with that person. I'm not saying that you wouldn't work out as a couple; I'm merely giving you my suggestion from my own experience and knowledge.

Being honest with the other person will also allow you not to get too seriously or too deeply into the relationship before you are ready, thus allowing you to take the time needed when you want some space. You are going to battle yourself a bit while healing, and having some alone time to process your feelings without outside distractions will be needed on occasion. If they know what's going on, they will be much more accepting of this than if they are kept in the dark. If the other person doesn't know what's happening or why you need some space, they will assume it's because of them or that you're losing interest. This isn't fair to the other party and it won't do either of you any good, so just be upfront about it and you will have more success.

I think some people might avoid telling someone they are going through a divorce because they are afraid they will be perceived as a failure. This is not the case, and you shouldn't be embarrassed by life's challenges. Most people will see that you have the ability and strength to follow your heart. The fact that you were in a marriage makes it clear that aren't afraid of commitment. If you're going through a divorce but you're still out there trying to meet someone new, you clearly aren't afraid to pursue your own happiness. View this part of your life as a positive experience and so will others.

UNDERSTANDING ADDICTION TO EMOTIONAL DRAMA

When someone in a relationship has been left, they can feel like they have been abandoned - left by their partner as though they meant nothing to them at all. This may have happened to you in the past as well and could still be affecting you with your current and future relationships. The reason I have included this in the chapter of self-awareness is that I feel it's a big part of knowing yourself and being able to select or pursue the correct partners going forward.

If you have gone through heartbreak in the past from being left by your partner, then you may associate the feeling of heartbreak or abandonment with feelings of love. This may also have happened with you if you had this happen with a parent or your parents. If one of your parents was not a big part of your life, then you may associate those feelings of abandonment with feelings of love also. This can lead you into pursuing people that are emotionally unavailable.

This can become somewhat of an addiction for people that have been abandoned in any kind of relationship, a rush that you get when someone gives you heartbreak. I have even heard this referred to as "abandon-holism." It can be viewed the same as some of the other addictive "isms," such as workaholism and alcoholism, but instead of being addicted to a substance, you are addicted to the emotional drama of heartbreak.

When someone is addicted to the emotional drama of heartbreak, they will pursue someone that they are insecure about in order to keep producing certain chemicals that are associated with feelings of love. If you are unable to recognize this and be aware of it, it can be a dangerous and never-ending loop. I've seen this in some of my friends and I've even seen it in myself. I was never treated poorly or abandoned by any of my parents, but I learned it from having my heart broken on more than one occasion.

You don't necessarily have to have been abandoned by a parent. If one of your parents treated the other one poorly or was emotionally unavailable towards the other one, then you may view that as normal or think that is what love is supposed to look like. This, combined with being heartbroken by a partner, can cause you to have an addiction to emotional drama and confuse you about what real love should look like.

This is a behavior that you need to know about, or you could end up wasting many of your premium years chasing the wrong types of people. It isn't easy admitting your faults to yourself and owning up to them, but being aware of this and not falling into your own trap will only be something that your future self will thank you for later. Of course, if you do find that you have some abandonment issues, you will have to create a change within yourself to pursue a different type of person than you're used to.

The hardest part about pursuing a different type of person is that you may not feel attracted to them. This was also another one of my problems. Have you ever asked yourself, "Why am I constantly meeting the wrong type of person?" or "Aren't there any good people left in this world?" Maybe it's because you are constantly going for the wrong ones. I'm sure some of us know we are attracted to the wrong types, but we just don't know why. Well, now you have some insight on why that may keep happening to you, and hopefully that can help you to better understand your loss of attraction to people that may be the right type of person for you to pursue.

Before I had heard of abandon-holism, I knew that I was dating the wrong types of people, so I actively tried to date a different type. Whenever I did this, however, I found myself running into a subconscious wall and losing attraction. I may have been interested in the person right from the get-go, both physically and emotionally, but it didn't seem to matter. I still lost my attraction to them. Therefore, it's imperative to be aware of _why you're feeling this way, and not just keep trying to meet person after person until you run out of options.

If you know that the person you are dating is a good person, and you were attracted to them at the beginning but then lost your attraction after a few dates, it's a good idea to give that person a few more dates to be certain and see if it's only the lack of emotional drama that's making you feel the lack of attraction towards them. It's quite possible that your loss of interest isn't because of them, but is your own issue. You might just find that this is the right person for you after all.

People that are dealing with abandonment issues are also easy prey for the narcissistic type and it may not be you that's pursuing them, but the other way around. Narcissistic people are professionals at picking out people that they can take advantage of and manipulate. They are also very emotionally unavailable and can seriously disrupt your life. If you don't know how to identify a narcissist, then I suggest reading a book on them. There is a ton of information on them and it's a great way to identify and avoid them.

Because I have dated a narcissist, I am more aware of what to look for and how to see red flags early on. If you are attracted to the emotionally unavailable type, then chances are you may have already dated a narcissist as well. As you can now see, being aware of whether you're addicted to emotional drama is a crucial step, not only to avoiding the wrong types, but also to taking a step in the right direction of finding true and lasting love.

CHAPTER 5: MOVING ON FROM YOUR PAST

Now that we've gone over how to deal with much of the healing process, we can we start looking at moving on from your past. This can be a difficult step, because it involves letting go of your past and potentially finding new love. Let me reiterate that the healing takes time, and you need to keep practicing the information in the previous chapters repeatedly until you feel it's time for you to move on. You will know when it starts to feel right and your emotions and feelings start to stabilize.

When you look back and think of your previous partner, how does it make you feel? Do you still have resentments towards them or the relationship? If you do, then keep going through the emotions in the chapter "Embracing Your Emotions" until you're able to look back and feel like you are content and ready to move forward. You should be able to look back at your past partner and accept that you loved them, valued the time that you had together, received some benefits from the relationship.

You should be able to have positive thoughts towards your memories with them. You might still have a few negative thoughts or memories, but those thoughts shouldn't be able to control your emotions anymore. This chapter is going to deal with breaking your attachment with your past partner. As I mentioned earlier, when you are doing some of the things that you used to do with your ex-partner, they can bring up feelings of familiarity.

Familiarity is not to be confused with love. A psychological definition of familiarity is "a generic feeling in which a situation, event, place, person or object directly provokes a subjective feeling of recognition which we then believe to be a memory. As a result, we recognize _it._" Basically, what that means is that when we go somewhere or do something familiar that we may have done with a person from our past, that experience can trigger a memory and generate a feeling referred to as familiarity. We think of that person when we see something, go somewhere or do something that we used to do with that person.

Familiarity can be a difficult thing to break, and it is something that time will help you with. Also, the more you create new memories, the more your old memories will fade. Try to get out there and continue doing the things that you love. This will also increase your chances of meeting someone with similar interests and hobbies. It's important to live your life the way that you normally would, even if you don't have a spouse or a partner. You may find that there are things that you've wanted to do that you haven't done in years, or have never done but always wanted to.

For myself, I ended up doing a lot more traveling than I used to. I explored new places I had never been and met all kinds of people. I was also going through a career change at the same time that I decided to start traveling more, so it was like a whole new chapter in my life. I ended up doing some traveling solo, which was out of my normal comfort zone. It forced me to come out of my shell more in order to meet new people. I found that I had no problems getting to know people and that people found me quite amicable. This made me happy and more open to meeting even more people. After all, the more friends we have in this world, the better!

Another thing I came to realize was that I had lost my sense of humor as a result of my past relationship. I was always tip-toeing along in my past and trying not to make any waves, and the result was that I had lost a bit of who I was. I had changed from who I wanted to be and who I should be. We all make changes or sacrifices to try to improve the relationship or meet a middle ground sometimes, but we should never change who we are as people.

This was something I now knew and would be aware of in the future if I was to enter a relationship again. As it turned out, I was quite a funny guy and I really enjoyed making other people laugh. I had forgotten what that felt like. Even my friends started to notice that I had improved my sense of humor and told me things like, "I wondered why you lost your sense of humor, but I didn't want to say anything." I used to think to myself, "Why on earth wouldn't you tell me that before?"

Having my sense of humor back also made it easier for me to attract women. I was never over the top with my sense of humor, but when you use just the right amount of humor, combined with some wittiness, it can be quite attractive for women. The same goes for attracting men if you are a woman. It doesn't matter if you're a man, woman, straight or gay, a sense of humor is attractive to anyone, because when you create laughter, it's contagious and makes the people around you feel enjoyment. Who wouldn't be attracted to that?

So, if you have a trait that you have let go of or have buried inside during your past relationship, then embrace it and let it shine through. It's who you are, and people will love it just because you're being yourself. Just make sure you aren't overdoing something or being obnoxious about it. Harness your power, my son! A little goes a long way! Use your self-awareness to read the people around you and see how they are reacting to you. If they are encouraging it and seem to be magnetized towards you, then you know you're on the right track. If they seem to be getting a bit annoyed or are kind of just giving subtle smirks, then back off a little and let them show you their own personalities some more. Make them prove why you should be interested in them, and ask them a few questions about themselves.

If you're the type of person that doesn't have any problems meeting others and talking to people you don't know, then great, if you know what you're doing. If you're the type of person that's a little more shelled-off, then try getting yourself out of your comfort zone. Sometimes this can be difficult for someone who has been in a long-term relationship. Later, I will cover ways for you to get yourself out there and become more confident in yourself and to become more approachable yourself. For now, just know that meeting new people is healthy and helps you with moving on and creating new memories.

It's also great for developing your people skills. When you meet one new person, and you end up maybe hanging out with them, you've now opened yourself up to their friend group. That may be dozens of people, who, in turn, may open you up to dozens of new experiences. It's a compounding effect and will have a positive impact on your life. Just remember, you still have the right to be picky with your friends group, and I highly recommend that. You want to make friends only with the type of people that are going to add value to you and your life.

If you're making friends with people that drain you or bring you down, then they aren't your friends. You are the CEO of your own life, and you control all who enter it. Now is when you need positive branches of friendship, and not someone who is going to pull you down. It's okay to have friends that are going through a tough time as well, but you know the types of people that I'm talking about. These are the types that aren't interested in your problems and constantly have baggage, but don't do anything about it. When you have your own problems, you don't need to entertain people like that.

That's not to say you need to be rude to these people or give them a snotty attitude; just distance yourself from them. This goes for the friends you already have too. A lot of times the type of people who can constitute a drain on your life can also be quite persuasive. This is usually a technique they have developed to get what they need from other people. If they are true friends, they will show you the respect that a true friend should and won't try peer-pressuring you for their own fulfillment.

Let's get back to being able to break your attachment to your ex-partner. One thing to keep in mind is that when someone has a major attachment to someone, it can be from something that the person was giving them, such as providing attention in a certain way, or giving the other person love and making them feel accepted. Strong attachments can be the result of some sort of emotional need you were getting met from that person that you weren't giving to yourself. If your ex made you feel accepted and loved and then you broke up those feelings of love and acceptance, then those feelings tend to be relinquished. This can leave you with a giant void, making you feel empty, lost and even craving that person.

Just like everything else, this will take a bit of work and a bit of time. As I've been saying throughout this book so far, there are many stages, and it's going to take some changes on your part, and some time. But with a little bit of work and commitment from your end, you will have your happy ending. If you've gotten to the part of moving on from your past, then most of the hard work has already been done, and it will only get easier for you from here on. You may have small relapses or moments of weakness from time to time, but I can assure you that you will be in a far better place and looking forward to your future.

So now that we know that having an attachment to someone is caused by a void in your own emotions that was being fulfilled by your partner, we can start looking at how to fix it. Try to figure out which emotions or feelings of comfort you received from your ex-partner. Did they show you love? Did they provide emotional support when you were trying something new? Did they say you looked good all the time and make you feel desirable? Perhaps they were very encouraging to you and always pushed you to do your best. Maybe they didn't do any of these things, but then you might be wondering why you were married or in a relationship with this person at all Well, the key is to really hunker down and analyze how they made you feel and what voids they were filling that you weren't already dealing with yourself. Figure out what needs you have that they were meeting for you.

If your ex was giving you feelings of constant love that you weren't already giving yourself, then you need to love yourself more. If they were supportive, and encouraged you to try new things or to get out of your comfort zone, then encourage yourself more and push yourself to promote change within. If they made you feel worthy, then give yourself more self-worth. It sounds simple I know, but really, that's what you need to do.

There's an old saying that states "You can't change how you feel," but this isn't a true statement. You can. I repeat - you can! You can control your emotions and how you feel about yourself. Remember how earlier I was telling you that it's important for both parties to be happy and have self-worth before they enter a relationship? Well, this is exactly why it's so important. When you are both self-worthy and happy, you won't rely on the other person to fill your own personal void, thus putting less strain on the relationship and therefore increasing the success rate of it. Also, if you're the type of person who is a bit controlling, you will be less likely to want to be controlling towards them in the relationship because you won't be so dependent on them to make you feel safe and worthy or to fill your own emotions. It's truly a win-win when you are both emotionally self-reliant.

When you do end up meeting someone that you want to have more than just an overnight fling with, look for these qualities in them as well. If you spend a few dates with them and start seeing that they are already becoming clingy or dependent on your attention, then try to be observant of it and see the warning signs. They are lacking something within themselves and are looking at receiving it from you.

Of course, no one is perfect, and most people do need to work on themselves in one way or another, but you can usually distinguish people who need a lot of work from those who need only a little. Also, try to watch for overly confident or overly dependent individuals as well. Sometimes people that are extremely independent and don't need anyone in their lives telling them what to do or how to do it can be masking or covering up for their own insecurities or another issue within themselves. Often it can be hard to get these types of people to become sympathetic or reason with them in a relationship. I mean, when it comes down to it, let's face it, if you find a person that you are crazy about then you are going to want to date them and please do so, just don't throw caution to the wind when it comes to heeding the warning signs.

DON'T LET YOUR PAST HOLD YOU HOSTAGE There comes a time where you may need to realize that you are just focusing too much on the past. Of course, you need to recognize what happened and deal with the past, but don't let it hold you back from having an amazing future. Some people can dwell more than others, so try not to let this be you.

If the past keeps coming up and you're still having a hard time letting go, then try to recognize it. I find that when people aren't the ones that did the breaking up, but rather the ones who were broken up with, it can be harder and take longer to let things go. This especially goes this way when their past partner has already gotten back out there and met someone new. This is because they feel abandoned and that they were unimportant and easily replaceable.

This isn't the case. Some people are just better at moving on than others, and some people are also just less emotional than others. Your ex-partner also may be trying to move on and bury their emotions rather than dealing with them properly. A lot of people will try to move on before they are ready, but that doesn't mean they will be happy or successful in the end. Just remember, you are taking the right steps and in the end, you will be happy.

Just as we discussed with familiarity, seeing something or doing something that you did with your ex can bring up uncomfortable and painful emotions. What you need to realize is that it's not the universe against you. It's not some mystical force that is playing "that song" on the radio that reminds you of your ex-partner or that you are being tortured and punished by having to drive past your old neighborhood where you lived with your ex.

It's you that is relating all these things to your ex, and it's you that makes the connection between driving down a street and thinking negative thoughts about your past relationship. It's not the objects or the scenarios, it's the meaning that you are giving them. The good news is that you can change the meaning that you are giving them at any point in time. Of course, dealing with your past negative emotions will help you with this, but also just try enjoying what it is about those things you liked in the first place.

Maybe "that song" has a good beat or it says something about love that you like and agree with. Try to enjoy what it is that originally made you love it, rather than changing the station every time it comes on. It's okay if driving through your old neighborhood gives you a bad feeling in your gut, but maybe that's the way for you to get to your job. Rather than driving a different route, try to remember why you lived there in the first place and what made you enjoy it. Maybe it's just an attractive or interesting area.

Your past isn't going to be easy to deal with. If it were, you wouldn't be reading this book. But that doesn't mean you need to let it hold you hostage or control your future. Take charge of your past, and take charge of your emotions. Acknowledge them, deal with them, and control how they make you feel. Take your negative emotions and gut feelings and spin them into positive ones. That's easier said than done, but with some effort, it's completely doable.

UNFOLLOW YOUR EX FROM SOCIAL MEDIA Unfollowing your ex and deleting them from your social media is something I would highly suggest. It's not always the easiest thing to do when you may have had so many memories and photos together. I suggest storing your photos and events onto a separate USB drive and putting it in a memories box, if you have one.

It's just too difficult to move on when you are still following your ex. Who wants to see photos or posts from their ex moving on and looking happy with someone else, especially when social media revolves around showing the best of situations rather than the hardships? Unfollowing them and deleting your photos will help you move on and prevent you from dwelling on the old times. Also, when someone new of interest comes along, they won't want to see pictures of you with your ex.

If you are the one that did the breaking up, then you may have some hate or resentment come your way from your ex, but taking this step is a part of acceptance, and eventually they will do the same if they haven't already. Seeing each other living day to day will only cause each other hurt. If you want to take it in baby steps, then try unfollowing their news feed instead of unfriending them. This will just prevent you from seeing all their posts.

If you see a post of your ex with someone else of the opposite sex, it's a natural reaction to sometimes think the worst. They could just be a friend, but you would not know that and you might come up with your own stories or scenarios of their situation. It's just plain easier and less hurtful to take the steps to prevent these kinds of things from happening.

CHAPTER 6: GETTING BACK OUT THERE

I wouldn't suggest jumping straight back into a relationship as your next step, but now is the time to be receptive to meeting new people and possibilities of dating. Keep your eyes open for people that might interest you, or if someone is interested in going on a date with you and you're attracted to them, then go for it! Going on dates will be healthy for you at this point and will help you further break the attachment with your ex. There are lots of great people out there. and you're now in a lucky position to venture out and start meeting some of them without being in a relationship.

Dating is an important step after a long-term relationship. Take the time to value your freedom before getting heavily involved with someone again. This is a unique opportunity for you to be picky and choose the mate that you want to be with and that you feel your best to be around. People talk about the pressures of dating and how it can be a super pain in the ass going through the process. Well, I'd be lying if I didn't tell you that the dating world can be frustrating at times, but try to see the positive in it.

My sister-in-law gave me some great advice about this. I was feeling frustrated and pressured that I couldn't seem to find someone that I liked for more than a few dates. I just couldn't meet anyone that I visualized spending the rest of my life with. My sister-in-law said to me, "Ryan, you're going to meet someone again and wish that you enjoyed this time that you have now, just having fun and dating. Just enjoy being single and selfish for a while. You deserve it." Single and selfish? I thought about this for a while. The more I thought about it, the more I liked it. She was right!

Following this new way of thinking, I really started to enjoy the dating scene again. My thinking before was that I had a timeline and needed to catch back up with where I was in my previous relationship. All I was doing was laying pressure on myself and giving into my fear that I might not meet someone. This was also making me consider lowering my standards or sacrificing something that I wanted in someone. This was the wrong way of thinking and wasn't going to get me to the place that I wanted to be.

I had no wife to worry about, no commitments, no one to be responsible for except myself. I had total freedom to do whatever I wanted. I had the right to be selfish with my time and selfish with what

I wanted in a future partner. This kind of thinking made a huge weight lift from my shoulders, and I began really enjoying just meeting new people and being open to friendships or other opportunities. How lucky was I to be able to do this in my life? Now that I was a bit older and wiser from my previous marriage, I had the right to be choosier and use my past experiences and new knowledge to help guide me through these new experiences.

I was now much more self-aware than I used to be, I knew what to look for in a potential partner and I knew what made me happy in life and how to just be myself. On top of that, I had conditioned myself to show "qualities" and "proofs" that people look for in a potential partner, and therefore I had the right to wait for someone who could show me those same qualities and proofs in return. I will go over how you can condition yourself the same way to attract your potential partner as well, but once you do, be aware that you will attract a lot of new prospects that form deep attractions towards you. This is something you need to learn how to control and be selective with. It's not an easy task trying to explain to someone that you aren't interested in them when they've already become seriously attracted to you.

There are many ways of getting back in circulation and meeting potential future partners, and your age, the type of relationship you're looking for (short-term, long-term, or whatever) and where you live will help determine where you look for them or decide to spend your free time. Of course, there are the usual, you know, night-clubs, bars, coffee shops, online dating sites, grocery stores, pretty much you-name-it, and there's somewhere you can potentially meet someone of interest, but basically there are two types of ways: _virtual_ and _physical._

I would suggest using both methods so that you can increase your odds and keep your standards as high as possible. The more ways you use to meet people, the better your chances of successfully finding the right person for you. Also, you might not have too many single friends to hang out with, and you aren't going to want to get back out there on your own.

VIRTUALLY It's not exactly fun to go hit up a bar when you're solo or sitting at a table for one in a restaurant. Therefore, many people decide to just go online and scope out profiles instead. It's just a lot easier as a first step and is less invasive. Virtual dating has both positives and negatives. It can be a big positive for people who live in a rural area where there aren't that many places to go out. Also, it makes it easy to set your dating goals.

If you want a short-term fling, then you can just set your preferences to that and it will automatically match you with other people looking for the same thing. If you want long-term, then you will only be matched with people seeking long-term relationships. It gives people a way of being honest and upfront about what they want from the beginning, rather than wasting a conversation with someone in person and getting your hopes up, only to find that your mating goals don't match up.

Another benefit of online dating is that it doesn't take much effort. Once you have a profile written and some pics up, you can literally just be sitting around in your underwear and sipping back on a glass of wine while scrolling the internet for potential mates. There are also tons of options for dating apps out there: Tinder, Plenty of Fish, Bumble, Match.com, and many others. Another thing to think of is that the virtual method is a lot cheaper. Most of the dating apps nowadays are free or have a minimal cost, and you don't have to be out ordering food or drinks in an establishment.

I'm all for the online thing as well, but online dating has its downsides too. My personal preference was to meet people in person while I was out and about. It was just way more appealing to me, as there weren't any tricks or games that way. Nothing is worse than seeing someone's photo online and then meeting them in person and they don't look like they are even the same person, or they look ten years older than in their photos. It will help you just see who's available in the age group that you are looking for. Depending on where you live will determine how high that you can set your standards and what your success rate will be.

If you live in a busy city with a two to one ratio of women to men, then obviously, your chances of success will be a lot higher and your standards can be high. If you live in the back country somewhere and there's only one coffee shop and a local saloon to socialize in, then your selection and chances of meeting the type of person you want will be a lot less, so your standards will have to be lower.

Whatever the case and wherever you live, I will help you display the best side of yourself so you can have the highest standards available to you. Also, if you live in an area where the odds aren't in your favor, consider moving somewhere where the odds are better, if it's possible for you to do that. It's not easy to pick up shop and move somewhere else, especially if you own a local business or are established in your career down the street, but this is *your* life and you only get one, so do whatever it is that you need to do to be happy and give it your best shot.

PHYSICALLY Just like virtually pursuing a mate, physically pursuing one also has positives and negatives. If you're the type of person that is very confident in yourself and is good at meeting new people, then you may want to consider putting your skills to the test in person rather than the internet. This is a great way for you to show your qualities and proofs out in public and in person.

When you're trying to advertise yourself online it's more difficult for people to see what an amazing personality you have, but when you're standing in front of them and engaged in a conversation, it's much easier to create a connection with them and show off some of your personal traits. That's something that works both ways, and it will help you determine what a person is like before you commit to a date with them. It gives both sides a chance to show their best sides to each other, unless one of you isn't interested in the other.

Sometimes, even if a person is interested, they won't show you their qualities or will play hard-to-get, in which case you must be able to detect that and use a higher level of game. Or the person may not be into you at all and you will have to be able to pick up on that and back down. We will go over how you can tell the differences shortly, so don't worry about that for now. At this point I just want to describe the types of ways to meet people when you're getting back out there.

Another thing that benefits you when physically meeting someone is that you get a chance to feel someone's energy. Energy plays a huge part in attraction. Whether you think you give off energy or not, believe me, you do. One of the downsides to having to use the physical method is that it takes a lot more effort. You must decide where you are going to go that night, shower and get ready, drive or walk there, and, of course, it involves more of a cost because obviously, you're going to go somewhere that you can have a drink or a coffee, eat, or whatever it may be. Also, you won't know if a person is even single or not and available to date until you talk to them.

And then, even if they are single and open to dating, they may not be looking for the same dating goals as you. And watch out for the ones that pretend they are single by giving you signs just to see if they are still desirable, and then when you go over and engage them in a conversation, you get suckered by an angry boyfriend or pissed girlfriend that was in the bathroom and comes back to see you hitting on their partner.

Regardless of the method you decide to start with, it all comes down to a physical interaction in the end anyway. You can't just sit on the internet and, when you finally agree to a date with someone, push a magic button to zap them through the screen of your laptop. You may have to hone your skills and do some work on yourself before going straight for the physical approach.

CHAPTER 7: BUILDING CONFIDENCE WITHOUT ARROGANCE

CONFIDENCE IS REAL A great deal of information is available on how to build self-confidence, a quality that plays a large role in getting the attention of someone you are trying to attract. You may be a very confident person in your day-to-day activities, and quite possibly when you were in a long-term relationship, but now that you're in the position to meet new people again you may find that your confidence has diminished. The reason for this is that you're involved in something that you haven't done for a while. The length of time it's been since you were last on the singles market will play a role on how much your self-confidence has changed.

Perhaps you are the type of person that has just always had low self-confidence and needs to build it from scratch. That's okay, and once you understand more about how it works, there's hope for you as well. The thing with self-assurance is that you can't pretend to have it when you really don't. Those of you that have low self-confidence may already know what I'm talking about if you've tried to fake it before.

Some people who are only pretending to be self-confident can come across as overly confident or arrogant, which is also an indication of low self-assurance. Women are especially intuitive about a man's poise. If you are only 90% confident, they will pick up on the 10% of you that isn't. Self-confidence is just something that must be real in the sense that you are assured in what you are doing and how you feel about yourself.

WHAT IS CONFIDENCE? Let's look at how self-confidence works and how simple it can be. When you do something that has repeated success and proven results, you will achieve a certain level of optimism that you will continue to have the same results in the future. For example, if you go to work tomorrow and know that you are going to do your job properly, it's because you've been doing your job for a while and know what you're doing through repeated success. It's something you know, trust, and have already proven to yourself and the others around you. This is the root of self-confidence.

Let's say instead that you're starting a new job tomorrow, something that you have never done before. What if yesterday you were a plumber and tomorrow you go into work and need to install some electrical wiring on a house? What would that do to your confidence level? Well, for starters. you'd be deathly afraid of frying yourself or burning the whole house to the ground. Obviously, you wouldn't switch from being a plumber to an electrician overnight, but this is simply an example to illustrate my point. Your confidence level would dramatically decrease because you would be put into a position where you wouldn't be sure of what you're doing and wouldn't have a history of proven results.

That may be true, but let's say that over time and with proper training, you work at being an electrician and prove to yourself that you can wire a house properly. Your confidence level would gradually increase the more that you do it and continue to prove your ability to yourself and the others around you.

The same thing goes for anything that you do in life. When you were a child and were learning how to ride a bike, you had low confidence and maybe needed to use training wheels, but after time has passed and the training wheels have come off you don't even give it a thought. You just jump on your bike and ride off without the slightest sign of low confidence. When you have been in a relationship for a long time and haven't had to be out meeting new people, just as if you haven't ridden a bike for years, you will have a lower level of confidence in yourself until you give yourself some repeated successful results again.

HOW TO BUILD CONFIDENCE Unfortunately there are simply no short cuts to building self-confidence. You literally just should do whatever it is that that makes you feel unsure about yourself until you increase your level of confidence. Many people who are quite self-assured when meeting men and women are that way simply because they've done it so often, and through trial and error they have built their confidence levels. There are no gimmicks, just efforts to gain this for yourself. Being unhappy with their physical appearance or feeling embarrassed about a particular part of their body can dramatically affect their self-confidence as well. It's quite natural and quite common for a person to do this to themselves. One thing you can do to correct this situation is to admit it to yourself. If you don't like your nose. then don't try to mask it or hide it. Just acknowledge to yourself that you don't like your nose. If your ears stick out more than you like, accept your feeling and don't try to hide it. It's okay if you don't like a part of your body.

I will let you in on a little secret. Everyone has a part of their body that they like the least. The best thing you can do is embrace it and accept it. Yes, of course people can get nose jobs or get their ears pinned, and if that's what you want to do, then go do it. But we were all born unique and special, and we all have something about us that is different from anyone else. We all have special signatures about ourselves that can distinguish us from the other lemmings around us.

I will give you an example of how embracing your physical traits can be sexy. I've always been an avid boater. In the summertime that's something I love doing, and I also enjoy sharing this activity with my friends and loved ones. One particular day, I was going boating with group of girlfriends that come out on occasion, and they happened to bring a female friend along that I hadn't met before. This girl had something that was noticeably unique about her, and no, I'm not going to talk about the size of her breasts in a bikini. It was her ears. They weren't huge or anything, but they stuck out quite a bit. Actually, a lot.

Of course, physical appearance is the first thing people notice before they get to know someone, so that was the first thing I saw. When you think about it, I noticed her before anyone else because of her ears. She had something unique about her that I saw over and above anyone. Whether it's a good thing or a bad thing is irrelevant at first; let's just talk about the fact that she was more noticeable. She had an advantage over her peers by having a pronounced physical feature that stood out from the others.

As our day went on and we enjoyed some sunshine and conversation, I got to know her a bit. One thing I noticed is that she wasn't trying to hide her ears at all. She seemed proud of them. You would maybe expect someone to be somewhat shy of them or try to hide them by wearing their hair down or be insecure and try talking from beside you rather than head-on or something, but not this girl. She loved herself and it showed. She obviously did not give two shits about whether her ears stuck out or not.

This made me attracted to her, the way that she was totally confident about herself, but without being overly confident and arrogant. She just was who she was, and it happened to be that she was a great person to talk to and a lot of fun. By the end of the day, the characteristic I became most attracted to, besides her personality, was her ears and how she was so confident about herself. I barely even noticed the other girls that were on my boat and was completely drawn to her instead.

This is an example of how something that you may be insecure about or find unattractive about yourself can be used to your advantage and even become the most attractive thing about you. There are actually quite a few people with physical disabilities that end up becoming motivational speakers. This is because they've embraced their disabilities and endorsed a positive and confident attitude about themselves and ended up being inspirational to other people.

The bottom line is that if you want to become self-confident, you need to embrace who you are and you need to find a way to be happy with yourself and like everything about yourself. Once you have that, you will become more self-confident and you will find that you can put your efforts into other things that are important when meeting new people, rather than wasting time and energy being worried about yourself and what other people think. As I mentioned earlier, gaining self-confidence will take a bit of work, but through time you will gain this. Not only do experience and being happy with yourself help gain self-confidence, but so does knowledge.

By simply reading this book you are probably already gaining knowledge about self-confidence and becoming more aware of what it is and how to build it up. The more you read, the more knowledge you will obtain and the more confidence you will gain in yourself, knowing that you have guidance. There are, of course, lots of other books out there dealing with self-confidence, so if you still find it difficult or slow to improve, think about picking some up and doing some more reading on the topic. They may even give you advice about trying to look your best to raise your confidence. And that brings us to our next chapter.

CHAPTER 8: ELEVATING YOUR ATTRACTIVENESS

Appearance is important, and anyone who tells you otherwise is lying to you. Whether we like it or not, a good haircut, proper fashion, and good grooming habits all play a role in how others perceive us. We all know that people only take a few seconds to form a first impression of you before they get to know you. If their first impression is negative, then you may never get a chance to get to know them at all. That's just the way the cookie crumbles. Nothing makes you feel better than knowing that you look good.

You know that feeling you get when you just got the perfect haircut or maybe you bought a piece of clothing that just seems to fit perfectly, almost as if it was made specifically for you? That's a good feeling to have, and did you notice how it also helped to boost your confidence? When you have that feeling (or energy), people around you pick up on that. You've probably noticed that before. When you are well kept, and appear to look after yourself, you increase your "level of value," and your chance of having a successful interaction and making a good impression on someone goes up.

When a man looks after himself, it shows a level of competency. It's quite simple really. if a man can take good care of himself, it shows that he may also have the capability to look after a woman and a family. If he can't even take care of himself and looks disheveled, then how is he supposed to look after a family? It also shows that he will be more likely to be accepted by her friends and the rest of society. No one wants to introduce a new man to their friend group and need to make excuses about why he is always wearing the same old clothes, never takes a shower and has holes in his running shoes.

A similar thing goes for women. When a woman is well groomed, and shows that she can take care of herself, it tells a man that she can care for their child or their children one day and she becomes more of an appropriate partner. If she looks like she doesn't care for herself at all, then how is she going to care for their offspring? Also, a man doesn't want to have to make excuses about a partner's appearance to his buddies. A guy wants to be proud of a partner's appearance and have his friends compliment him on his choice.

It may seem a bit sexist to put it in terms like this, but this is something that derives from prehistoric times between men and women. Yes, things are vastly different nowadays, but our subconscious minds still relate back to our core values. Women will still instinctively be attracted to a man that has good genes and can look after her and their children, and a man will automatically be attracted to a woman that has good genes and can look after their child. If a person chooses a partner because they are nice and will be kind to them, or merely because they have a steady job and make good money, without even considering attractiveness, then they are settling.

There are many ways to build your attractiveness and attract the partner that you really desire and truly deserve. You may just be dating for now, but when you find one that really stands out for you and they seem like they might have potential to be a lifelong partner, then at least you will be ready.

HAIR Good grooming habits start with your hair. No one is saying you need to be totally up to date or trying to make a new fashion statement with your hair. Just make sure that, if you have hair, you wash it regularly and groom it or style it in some way.

If you're a woman with long hair, then brush it, straighten it, or tie it back. If you're a man and have short hair, comb it, gel it, or use male hair product. Don't try to go crazy and set a statement like a spiked-up rock star, just go with something simple like a Caesar cut or side part. People will appreciate someone who looks neat and tidy rather than someone who walks out the door looking like they just woke up from bed or someone that has a hairstyle that looks like they're trying to get attention.

On the other hand, if you have a hairstyle that seems to work for you and is a bit different, then go for it, but maybe ask some friends how they think it looks on you. Make sure you ask the ones that you know will be honest to you, or, better yet, ask someone of the opposite sex.

FOR THE FELLAS Guys, if you're bald or like to have a shaved head look, then make sure it stays that way. There's nothing wrong with the bald look and many women find it quite sexy, including my girlfriend. Some of the hottest guys in Hollywood are bald, including Vin Diesel, The Rock, and Jason Statham. Just make sure that if you are bald on the top that you keep the rest of the hair on your head nice and short. Keep the sides shaved or buzzed short.

If you are going to have a beard, make sure that your beard is well groomed. Don't let it get long and out of control, keep it to a reasonable length, and make sure the edges are trimmed with your neck line shaved. As far as your eyebrows go (or in some cases maybe one eyebrow), don't be afraid to get out a pair of tweezers now and then, but for the love of God don't use a razor or straight blade. No one is saying that you need to shape them and make them all pretty, but if you have a unibrow, please do something about it.

As far as the rest of the hair on your body, just use your common sense. If you have a lot of body hair, then try to keep it as trimmed as possible. I don't shave my arm hair but I keep it somewhat trimmed, or it tends to just keep growing and growing. I also have dark hair, so it's more pronounced. If you have light hair you may not have to trim it quite as much. Lastly, get yourself a pair of nose trimmers if you don't have any. Nothing is worse than talking to someone and all you can concentrate on is a bunch of hair coming out of their nose. Very unattractive!

FOR THE LADIES Ladies, make sure to keep your eyebrows plucked and shaped properly. Please don't make them overly shaped or drawn on like the turn signal on a car. Just make sure they a looked after and shaped, so they still look somewhat natural. When it comes to any of the hair that needs waxing, then try to keep it waxed often enough that the hair isn't noticeable. Keep your legs waxed when you wear a dress or skirt, and if you have noticeably dark hair on your arms or face, then do your best to take care of it.

Also, let's not forget about nose hairs. Yes, we know that you have nose hairs too. Make sure, if you don't have a nose trimmer and need one, that you get one and use it. Next, make sure when you do your makeup that it's not overly done. Speaking from a man's perspective, we like it when a woman lets her natural beauty shine through. When someone cakes on a pile of makeup, we notice. Yes, even guys notice when there's too much foundation used or there's enough eyeliner to resemble a raccoon. Sure, put on some cherry red lipstick or let a certain feature stand out a bit, but be reasonable with the rest of it.

TEETH We will go over the importance of a smile in a bit, and teeth are also an important part of it. Not only are they important for appearance, but having good hygiene with your teeth is also directly related to the health of your heart. If you aren't one to look after your teeth and have a lot of plaque and calculus, then you can be more prone to heart disease. Brush your teeth regularly and floss regularly. A yellow smile can be very unattractive to someone, even if they are physically attracted to everything else about you. The same goes if you have bad breath. No one wants to talk with someone that smells like hot garbage.

No one is telling you that you need to go see an orthodontist and ask for braces or go through dental surgery. Just look after them. Hopefully you will have them for the rest of your life, so, why wouldn't you? If you don't have dental coverage, then at least get your teeth cleaned professionally once or twice a year. If you smoke or drink a lot of coffee and they are yellow, then go to your local store and pick up some whitening strips. Your smile is important and you're going to need to use it.

FASHION This one is important for both sexes. Fashion has always played a role in society for humans. Even back to very early times, clothing and fashion have been a major indicator of status and attributed to one's attractiveness. Many people are mistaken to think that women's fashion is more important than a man's. Even to this day, there are tribes in Africa that follow the traditional ways of their predecessors where the men must dress up and stand before the women to try to woo a possible mate. They also must perform traditional dances and songs, but don't worry, I'm not going to get into singing and dancing. You can go to a fine arts studio and take lessons for that.

When I say fashion, I don't mean that you should be ready to strut the runway in the latest Coco Chanel design, walking the streets in Christian Louboutin's newest footwear or ordering a coffee in a brand new Dolce & Gabbana suit, although that would be awesome. Just like our grooming habits, being dressed well shows that we can look after ourselves and therefore have the mental and physical abilities to look after a spouse, and children, so this is still very important when attracting a partner. Now you can spend hours trying to figure out the latest fashion online, but you will simply be wasting your time, and you don't need to go to that extent.

Just look around you. Do you have a friend that has always been fashionable? Pay attention to what they are wearing when you see them next. Maybe even ask them for a few tips. They would probably be flattered that you noticed that they put effort into their fashion. Do you have a favorite place that you hang out, like a coffee shop or maybe a bar or lounge where you go to enjoy a favorite cocktail? Take notice of the people in there that you might have seen before. Is there that one person that always seems to have people around them and always seems to be quite popular? Maybe there's that one guy who seems fashionable and always seems to have good looking women around him. Or maybe there's that one girl that seems to be well put together and always has good looking men approaching her. You know, the one you probably hate, LOL. Well take notice of that person and what they are wearing.

As a matter of fact, look at their whole façade. Look at their hair and how they groom themselves. See what type of clothes they wear and how they wear them. Now simply just rip them off! Now, I don't mean physically rip their clothes off, but copy fashion ideas from them. If they are hanging out in an establishment that you like to frequent often, then what they are attracting are the types of people that you like to be around and probably some potential partners for you.

If you like a certain type of person or environment, then you should take visual fashion tips from the person that has success in that same environment. If you are the type of person that likes to go to a trendy jazz bar where people dress in pressed pants and collared button-up shirts, then you probably won't have much fashion success if you're dressed that way in a biker bar or vice-versa. Dress for your preferred environment where you are attracted to the type of people that are there, but just make sure that you try to keep it simple and inviting. Just like make up, ladies, you don't want to overdo it and try to hide your natural self. And, guys, don't try to outdo the ladies. Keep it somewhat simple with some reasonable fashion sense, and make sure the clothes are somewhat fitted and you know what sizes to buy

yourself.

CHAPTER 9: LOOKING AFTER YOURSELF

Not only do you have to look after your emotions and feelings, you also must look after your physical well-being. Again, if you can't look after yourself, how are you going to look after your partner's needs? Physically looking after yourself shows that you can take care of yourself, and also shows that you can have the mental commitment needed for not only physical but also mental health. Since physically looking after yourself is a process that doesn't achieve results overnight, it shows that you are able to commit to something. This is good for someone who sees you as a potential partner.

REDUCING STRESS This one is easier said than done, as I'm sure we all know. There are so many factors that contribute to our stress levels in so many ways. We all have different reasons for accumulating stress in our lives, and depending on what kind of responsibilities we have, we will delegate the type and degrees of stress that we are up against.

Maybe you have children that are young and require a lot of help from you, or maybe they are at an age where they have commitments, such as sport activities and education, and they demand a large amount of your time to fulfill their own responsibilities. Maybe you have a very demanding position at work or you are responsible for many employees, or possibly you own your own business and it requires your full attention. Perhaps you have a position at work where your income barely meets your needs and you are stressed to make ends meet and need to constantly be working.

As you know, there are many contributing factors, and now that you've had to deal with a major breakup or divorce on top of things, your stress levels could be going through the roof. Therefore, reducing your stress levels is going to be so important now. You can read and take as much advice from this book as possible, but if you have extremely high stress levels and don't look after it, it's going to be difficult for you to apply any of the knowledge that I can give you. Also, others around you will be able to pick up on your negative energy, and it will be unattractive to them, and you may find it difficult to meet people.

The good news is we've already gone through some things that will help you with your stress, and we will be going over some more. Meditation was one that helps, but the biggest one was just being self-aware. Think about what is creating the most stress for you. The obvious one, of going through a breakup, can be dealt with just by being aware of how you're feeling and dealing with your emotions. Not only will you feel better every time you do this, but you will feel like a bit of weight has lifted each time you practice this exercise. This is your stress being reduced and coming off your shoulders a little each time.

This isn't just with your breakup, but also just being self-aware of all your emotions for whatever reason you have throughout your day. If you're angry at your boss or at a co-worker, use your new ability of being self-aware and think about why you're angry. Acknowledge that you are pissed off, then think about why you're pissed off and why it's making you feel that way. Then think about what you can do to improve or correct the situation, create a change in your emotion and move on from it. So, to simplify it, 1) Acknowledge your emotion, 2) Feel your emotion, 3) Think about why, 4) Create a change and, 5) Move on.

1) Acknowledge

2) Feel

3) Think

4) Change

5) Move on

GET SOME REST Getting the proper amount of sleep is very, very, very important. Did I mention how important this is? Yes, it's THAT important! It's important for just about everything. It helps build your attractiveness and physical appearance, expands your energy levels, reduces stress, improves mood, expands brain function, increases longevity of life, improves immune function and overall health, and even helps with weight loss.

Have you ever met a family member or a friend of yours and had them say, "Wow, you look tired!"? I'm pretty sure just about everyone has had a friend tell them that on more than one occasion, especially if you've had kids. Well, that's because they can tell just by looking at you. The main reason for this is that during sleep your body works to remove dead brain cells and blood cells and clears passages for new ones through synapses.

During sleep, your body also works at an elevated level to remove toxins and balance pH levels. If you're going to take anything from this chapter, let it be that you decide to get more sleep. That can be difficult to do when you're going non-stop all day and barely have time for yourself, but you need to make time. Try to get eight hours a day, every single day. You might not always get it, and maybe you will get only seven, but always try to aim for getting a solid eight hours of quality sleep.

QUALITY SLEEP It's not just the amount of time you lie in your bed, but it's the actual quality of sleep that really counts. The type of sleep that is most important to us is REM (rapid eye movement) sleep. REM sleep is the most crucial because it's the restorative part of our sleep cycle. There are four different kinds of non-REM sleep that our body requires before entering an REM stage. When we skip out on sleep or deprive our bodies from getting the required amount needed to achieve all levels of sleep, our body can change its cycle to obtain as much REM as possible.

Sometimes your body will skip the non-REM sleep and just go straight into an REM stage, thus going against the natural sleep cycle. Poor sleep cycles can result in poor concentration, grogginess and much more. This can also change the way that we dream. Researchers are still trying to discover the full purposes of why we need REM sleep and why we dream, but many researchers theorize that dreams are the way that the brain processes emotions, stress, information and memories.

There are many ways that you can obtain proper sleep. Here are some tips:

- Routine. Try to keep a regular routine. Make a consistent plan for when you go to bed so that you can get the required amount of sleep before having to get up for work. Your body will adapt to being regular and start becoming tired in anticipation before you're even in bed. The more consistent you become with your bedtime routine, the easier it will be to fall asleep and get the required amount of rest.

- Meditate. Incorporate meditation for 10 or 20 minutes before your regular bed time. This will help you relax and unwind from your day. It will also help you gain clarity and empty your mind of thoughts that can cause your mind to stir during bed and prevent sleep. It will "prep" your mind and body for a good night's sleep. Sometimes I almost get to the point where I'm falling asleep during meditation.

- Manage your caffeine. Try not to have any caffeine past the early afternoon. I personally cut my caffeine off after 3:00 p.m., but everyone is different. If you enjoy having a coffee or tea later in the evening, just make sure it's decaffeinated.

- Manage your alcohol. Research shows that drinking alcohol at night can reduce the amount of REM sleep that your body will get. Alcohol can make you fall asleep quicker and sleep more deeply for a while, but it reduces the amount of REM sleep you will have. And the more alcohol you consume before bed, the more pronounced these affects will be.

- Manage your eating. Don't eat any big meals before bed. Try to manage your eating throughout the day so you're not having dinner shortly before bedtime. If you like to have a snack in the evening, try to keep it a minimum of two hours before you hit the sack. If you're absolutely starving and need to eat something before going to bed, then try to have something light without dairy or carbs.

- <u>Don't work out late.</u> If you go to the gym, try to go straight after work or, if your schedule allows it, during the day some time. If you go too late in the day, your heart rate and endorphin levels may still be elevated and it can become difficult to sleep. It's not easy to fit everything we want into a day, but do your best to pre-plan and get a schedule going to work out earlier rather than later.

- <u>Limit electronics.</u> With all the electronics, we have around us, it can be hard to limit the use of them. The truth is that our electronic devices, such as TVs, cell phones, and laptops, give off a type of short wave blue light that prevents us from sleeping. We are meant to be awake during the day and asleep at night.

When you are looking at a screen that is emitting light, it can trick the mind into thinking it's still daytime and ultimately disrupt your regular sleeping cycle. Some phones have a setting that allows you to reduce the amount of blue light that is projected from the device at night time. My suggestion is not to look at it for at least an hour before your bedtime. Use this hour to read a book or work on yourself, or whatever you find enjoyable and relaxing that aids in sleep rather than hinders it.

- <u>Keep it cool.</u> Try not to keep your bedroom too warm. Having your bedroom too warm can be a large contributor to not having a good sleep. I also try to keep a window cracked a bit to allow fresh air into the room. This ensures that I'm not breathing in as much carbon dioxide and that my air quality is at its best. If you have an air purifier, then great; you're one step ahead of me.

Hopefully with using the tips above, you can improve not only the amount of sleep that you get, but also the quality of sleep. Having a good night's sleep will be something that adds quality and value to your life at all levels. And once you start getting a good night's sleep you will find it's something that you just won't sacrifice ever again.

WORK OUT Working out is something that is often aside due to a lack of time or the inability to commit. It's tough to get into or get back into exercise if you haven't done it for a while, yet it's so important. If you're not the type of person that works out and you absolutely will never go to the gym, then get some other kinds of exercise, whether it's going for runs, walking, or playing a team sport.

As I said earlier, going to the gym will not only show that you are physically fit, but it demonstrates that you are able to make commitments. Even if the commitment is to yourself, it still shows that you can commit and therefore you have a mental stability along with your physical stability. When a person is physically fit, that is very attractive to a prospective partner.

We've gone over how a person forms an opinion on you within seconds of seeing you, and when you are physically fit it's an added plus for you and will work as a benefit when meeting that person. It can even cause a sexual attraction just from a quick glance at someone that is fit, dresses well, and looks after themselves. This will give you an immediate advantage over everyone else around you.

Not only will being physically fit make you more attractive to your potential partners around you, but it will also make you feel good about yourself, raise your self-confidence, make you healthier and stronger, raise your energy levels, improve your sex drive and give you a "higher value" (which we will still discuss soon). There are just too many advantages to eliminate working out from this whole process.

There are many times in my life that I have been complimented about being in good shape, and it's always felt flattering and made me feel good about myself. If you're already fit and have an exercise routing, then you know what I mean, and I can bet that every hour you put in the gym working on yourself has been worth it.

Now, I'm not telling you that you need to hit the weights and become the next bodybuilding IFBB champion or women's physique winner, I'm just saying that you need to the gym a reasonable amount of times in each week. You can even start with going just one or two days a week for 45 minutes per workout. Once you slowly develop a routine, you will automatically become addicted to your body's natural release of endorphins, dopamine, and serotonin.

These chemicals are responsible for happiness, pleasure, and exhilaration. Dopamine is even associated with orgasms! People think working out is a much larger commitment than it really is, which is why it can be intimidating for some people, but it's not at all.

Maybe you're lacking a bit of confidence to hit the gym for the first time or to join that yoga class that you've always thought about, or a cross-fit program. Remember how we were discussing how to build self-confidence earlier? Well, one way was through knowledge. Maybe do some research on the internet and find some different workout exercises. Just try to keep it basic.

When I'm somewhat limited on time, I just keep my week of exercise basic. I keep it to pushing exercises one day, pulling exercises another day, and legs for the last day. You also don't have to push yourself that hard if you aren't going into a competition. Just get back out there. And you haven't ever been a gym person, but only because you've made excuses, then start now. What do you have to lose? It's the fastest way to feel good about yourself, reduce stress, and elevate your attractiveness.

EAT RIGHT If you've committed to most of the above ways of life then it only makes sense to add the final step: eating right. I'm not going to tell you that all you can have is chicken breast, yams and broccoli, and I'm not going to go into crazy diet routines or the latest and most popular fad diets, but what I will do is just give you some simple tips to follow. After all, if you're working out and not eating healthy, you're wasting a lot of your hard work.

- <u>Reduce sugars.</u> If you're trying to improve your eating habits and want to pick only one thing to change, reducing simple sugars would give the biggest bang for your buck. That stuff is a killer. There are so many reasons we shouldn't eat or drink simple sugars, but, as I said, I won't go into great depth. Just know that out of all the things our bodies need, we don't require any kind of simple sugar whatsoever. Getting rid of sugar altogether can be like coming off crack cocaine. Once you stop having it, you will realize how addicted you are to it. You don't have to cut it out entirely, but eliminate it as much of it as possible for maximum results. Have one pack of sugar in your coffee instead of two. Don't eat dessert after dinner. And absolutely don't drink any sodas. If you are drinking sugary soda drinks, you need to cut those out. They do all kinds of damage. If you like snacks, eat a healthy one without sugar in it. Make a valiant effort to substantially reduce your sugar intake and your body will reward you for it. I promise you this. The beginning is the hardest, but once you get past that, it gets easier and you will feel amazing.

- <u>Control your carbs.</u> Control the quantity of carbs and the types of carbs that you eat. Try to keep away from carbs that can be easily broken down by your body. If you don't know the difference between simple and complex carbs, then you may want to take a few moments to research it. Basically, simple carbs are more easily broken down and used as energy. You are better off eating more complex carbs as they are slower to break down and are packed with fiber and they will keep you feeling full for longer, thus reducing your cravings for more food.

-Some examples of simple carbs are: White bread, white rice, baked goods, fruit juice, milk, yogurt, honey, jam, and pasta made with white flour.

-Some examples of complex carbs are: Brown rice, potatoes, quinoa, beans, yams, bananas, broccoli, asparagus, cauliflower, whole wheat breads and pastas, and oatmeal.

- <u>Eat Healthy Proteins.</u> Eating protein is crucial for building and repairing muscle tissue, especially when you are active or working out. Now, there are lots of health nuts that would probably love to jump all over me and tell me what kind of proteins are healthy ones, so rather than telling you what you need to do, I will give you my suggestions.

Many people argue whether you should have plant-based proteins or animal proteins. Some people say plant-based is the only way to go and that animal-based will give you cancers and diseases. Others say there are essential substances in animal proteins that our bodies cannot live without and we will get sick if we only rely on plant-based proteins.

You are free to watch as many documentaries on Netflix about these two types of proteins as you wish. There's no shortage of them. My take on the whole thing is that I think it's healthy to create a balance between the two. I don't eat meat with all my meals, but when I don't, I increase the type of plant protein I'm having (like adding more kale) or I incorporate something like quinoa.

If I'm working out lots, I tend to eat more chicken, but I make sure that it's chicken breast and not thighs, which are fattier. Generally, I eat more meals with animal protein than without, but for one month out of the year I go on a strict vegetarian diet. When I do eat meat, I choose foods like chicken breast, white fish and occasionally lean cuts of red meat. When I eat plant-based, I choose foods like quinoa, kale, asparagus, pumpkin seeds, lentils, cauliflower and spinach.

- Reduce bad fats. Bad fats are foods that usually contain trans-fat, such as French fries, potato chips, fried foods, and fast foods. Avoid pre-mixed snacks and goods like cake mix, pancake mix and products that are partially hydrogenated. Make sure that even though you are eliminating bad fats, you are still eating good fats. Look for foods with omega-fats, like salmon, walnuts, Brussels sprouts, and avocados.

Unless you're a very self-disciplined person it will be difficult to follow the perfect diet to a tee, but try to do the best you can with it.

If you try to be too disciplined right away, eating right may be more be more difficult than slowly eliminating bad foods and bringing in good ones. Be fair with yourself and make gradual changes, and you will find that it's easier to eat healthy than you think. If you do change gradually, then you will be more likely to stick with it. After a bit of time you will notice that you don't even miss the bad foods, and in fact you will most likely prefer the good foods over the bad ones. You will also find that you like the new results in your body more than you liked eating all that shitty food.

CHAPTER 10: GETTING PERSONAL

The difficult part about meeting people nowadays is that we've become such a digital era that people have difficulties interacting in person rather than digitally, especially if you're a millennial. This is mainly due to digital devices like cell phones and laptops and all the types of social media out there, such as Facebook, LinkedIn, Instagram, and Snapchat. Of course, some of these can be a benefit to you, but when it comes to personal interactions with a prospective partner, they can be a disadvantage. And I'm not just talking about the person you wish to have a personal interaction with, I'm also talking about you.

It's not just social media either. It's also the way we operate on a day-to-day basis at work that has had a profound effect on the way we interact with other human beings. Every business out there has had to make changes over the years to keep up with the ever-changing technological world. If they didn't make any changes to keep up with technology, they would be left behind and forced to close their doors. People may think that the world of cell phones and e-mail has greatly improved communication, but what it has really done is improved the "convenience" of communication. It's made communicating easier, faster, and more efficient. What it hasn't done is improve the quality of communication.

At the age of 18 I was lucky enough to get my foot in the door with a company that was involved in a rapidly growing industry. It was a smaller company with a bit of a mom-and-pop style of operating, and at the time I didn't really notice or understand what I was getting involved in. All I knew was that I had to constantly work my butt off daily to make a paycheck. Through hard work and consistency, I slowly worked my way up through the ranks of the company. Then, years later, that company was purchased by a much larger corporation.

After the takeover, we had to adjust to how this larger, much more advanced company operated. We were given cell phones and desktops computers. We had to learn new company policies and procedures. I adapted to these new ways and just kept doing what I knew while working hard and consistent. Through proving myself, I kept moving through the ranks and became the top manager in my department, right under the operations manager and vice president of the region.

As the company grew, it became increasingly reliant on technology and technological devices to improve the convenience of communication. The company bought other companies up rapidly. If they had a major competitor, they would just buy them out and add their employees to the ranks with the rest of us. We opened branches across the country and eventually became an international company, buying up companies in new territory the same as we did in our own country.

With all the extra people being added to the company's payroll, we had to keep adopting ways of making communicating easier by improving technology and becoming more digital. Soon we had newer devices, and more of them. I often found myself leaving the office with a laptop computer, an iPad, and two cell phones (one for business and one for personal use).

The major problem with this is that everyone has become more digital not only at work, but also on a personal level at home. People look at laptops all day, and when they go into meetings they take their cell phones with them. When they get home, they are on their phones texting and looking at their social media. People have become very reliant on their devices and have also become addicted to them. The reason I say "addicted" is because when you hear that little "bing" on your phone and know that you just received a text message, your body releases the chemical dopamine. This is the same chemical that makes you feel good when you have a drink or do certain drugs.

With all the digital interaction, we have now, you can see why it would be more difficult to interact with people on a personal level. People have become what I like to call "data- oriented." People are in the data mode all day long, and when they get home they continue this data-oriented path.

Let's say your friend invites you to go out for a drink at a local social house, so you meet there over a beer or glass of wine. You talk about your day or what's going on in your single life. You look over and see someone that interests you. You want to go over and talk with them, but instead you sit there and continue your conversation with your friend. Time goes by and you keep telling yourself, "I will go over there in a bit," or "I can't think of anything to say right now." Eventually too much time goes by and they either leave or someone else strikes up a conversation with them and you miss out on the opportunity.

I once watched a friend of mine literally wait hours to talk to someone, but then he never did. I was wondering if I should help him, but I decided that I would rather watch what he did. He even asked me to help him strike up a conversation, but I told him he was on his own and that he had to do it. The main reasons he struggled with himself was because he had a lack of self-confidence and his brain was stuck in digital mode.

Has this ever happened to you? If it has, don't feel bad. This happens to a lot of people, and part of the reason is that you're still stuck in a digital mode. Sure, you have no problems talking with your friend because you already know them and aren't trying to start a conversation or think of something witty to say. When you're sitting in front of an electronic device all day and then want to have a witty conversation with someone, you're expecting your brain to change from a digital mode to an interactive mode.

Sometimes this switch can be difficult and can seem like a giant leap rather than a small step. You may not be aware of this, but hopefully I can help you move from a digital mode to a socially interactive mode whenever you require. Rather than trying to change directly from one to the next, you can create little baby steps for yourself until you teach yourself how to instantly move from one to the other. Of course, with it takes practice and a bit of work.

BABY STEPS Give yourself some small baby steps to get from a place of being in a digital made to a personal mode. You can practice this by simply asking a stranger a simple question. If you're on a lunch break and are walking down the street to grab a coffee, for instance, you can use this time to try something. You could try asking a person where the nearest coffee shop is. Sometimes people have a fear of rejection, but you're not asking a person on a date, you're only asking them where you can get a coffee. No one is going to tell you to take a hike or screw off, they are just going to tell you where the nearest coffee shop is. The worst response you will get is they might ignore you, or they might not know where the nearest coffee shop is.

It seems like such a small thing to do, but even such an easy activity will get you used to talking to someone in person that you don't know, rather than walking down the street with your head buried in your cell phone. Try this technique a few times and then add on to it. If they do tell you where the nearest coffee shop is, ask them if it's a Starbucks or some other coffee shop. Remember, you're not trying to pick someone up here, so don't act like you are, just be yourself. If they tell you it is a Starbuck's you can say something like, "Great! Starbucks is my favorite." If they seem like they don't care, then say thanks and keep walking. If they crack a smile and say it's their favorite too, then try to keep the conversation going. Maybe say, "That's awesome. I love their caramel macchiatos. What about you?" Of course, everything is based on how you deliver it. Try not to come across creepy. Keep it light and don't push it.

When you keep doing this, you are removing yourself from a digital mindset and into a personal one. You're also not trying to hit on the person either, so there's less pressure on your end, less fear of rejection, and, on top of that, you will come across as being less threatening to the other person. You can practice this type of exercise no matter where you are.

When you're in the coffee shop say "hi" to the person next to you. Ask them how their day is going. If you're in a grocery store, same thing goes. Say "hello" and be friendly and then walk away. When you're in a business meeting, instead of bringing your cell phone with you, leave it at your desk. While you're waiting for the meeting to start, ask the person next to you how they're doing. Get to know them on a personal level rather than just business. And when your meeting starts and your phone isn't sitting on the table, it shows that you care about listening to people and you aren't just there because you have to be.

Whenever you have someone that is willing to talk more, then go for it, but without being overwhelming or saying too much. The more you do this, the easier it will become for you to talk with people you don't know and the easier you will be able to change from digital mode to personal mode. If you want to up the ante, just start talking with people that you find attractive and would possibly be interested in dating, maybe someone you would be too nervous to talk with or ask a question. Be confident in yourself and be sincere. Just ask simple questions and keep it in your mind that you aren't trying to flirt with them. Even if someone does act snotty or says something negative to you, then just let it slide off. Don't let this stop you. It's just something personal in their own life and they have probably had a bad experience from someone being inappropriate towards them. Or it may be that they are full of themselves, and in that case, you don't want to talk to them anyway.

When you get yourself used to having a general non-threatening, friendly conversation with someone you find attractive or normally might fear talking with, it will really help you just to be yourself, and get you more in the flow of being in personal mode, and even help with your self-confidence.

Before you know it, you will find that it becomes easier to switch yourself freely from a digital mode into a mode where you can instantly speak with anyone you choose. You will also find that you may even become wittier in your conversations with people. Maybe next time you're out having a drink with a friend you won't be afraid to walk across the room and start a conversation with that someone that you find attractive.

CHAPTER 11: PICKING UP ON THE SIGNS

When you're out looking for a prospective partner, being able to pick up on the proper signs can be frustrating and daunting for some people. When I first started going out and looking for a possible mate, I had no idea what I was looking for. I would just go up to anyone I found attractive. Usually this would end up in failure on my end, until I started understanding the proper signals that people give off.

These can sometimes be subtle clues and sometimes they can be obvious, but, regardless, you need to know what you're looking for to act on them. If you're a man, then you will most likely have to give an action to get a reaction and read the sign. If you're a woman, then it's most likely the man that will give you the action, and it's how you react to this action that will enable him to see if you are approachable or not.

Since the beginning of mankind, it has always been up to the men to pursue the women. In the era of cavemen, it was the same. The man would find a woman that he liked, club her over the head and drag her by her hair back to his cave. Although the times have changed and women occasionally go after the man, it's still generally up to the guy to do the approaching. That is why signaling is important. In our society, single women like to be desired and chased and sometimes play hard-to-get. As time goes on, women tend to get sexier and sexier. They keep us on our toes with the latest fashion and have new techniques for wearing make-up and knowing what to do to increase their sex appeal. Because of this, men tend to put women on pedestals and can find approaching them difficult.

Through fear of rejection and the convenience of technology and dating apps, it seems that men are less and less likely to approach a woman that they find attractive. And when they do approach, if they are rejected or strike out, they are less likely to try again, or they may wait quite some time before approaching someone new. This is a shame, and if men understood how to read the appropriate signals, this would rarely happen.

To read the signals, you need to be able to trigger an appropriate reaction, and to trigger that reaction, you need to create an action. This goes for both men and women. This doesn't have to be anything substantial. It can be something very subtle, something no one around you would even notice, maybe as small as a smile and some eye contact. All you're trying to create is a simple reaction so you have something to read or pick up on. This will take the guess work out of whether a person is interested or open to further communication. It is a simple non-verbal way of communicating and will give you the confidence you need without wasting your time and/or creating yourself an embarrassment.

There are three ways that a person will react back to you. They can react with a *positive*, a *negative*, or a *neutral* reaction. You don't have to use a smile. You can go with something more forward, like waving your hand in the air or even pointing at them from a distance. You just need any action to create a reaction. The most important thing you need to apply is eye contact. This is because you need to be sure that they notice you and that they know it's them that you are throwing this action to.

You may seem like you're being a bit silly waving at a stranger from across a room, but this is where you need to let your confidence shine through. If you're too shy at first, then just use a simple smile or a nod. Just remember that the less action you give, the less reaction you will get, so you will need to be more skilled at being able to read that person's signals or signs.

Let's say you see someone you're attracted to, so you give them a smile and a nod while keeping eye contact. Here are the differences among the three reactions they will give you and how to read them:

- <u>Positive reactions.</u> If you smile at a person and they keep eye contact with you and smile back, this is a positive. If you smile and nod and they smile and nod back at you, this is a positive. If you point or give a little wave and they wave back at you, then it's on like Donkey Kong (that means very positive). Again, you can see that the stronger the action you give, the stronger the reaction will be, and therefore the easier it will be to read.

- <u>Negative reactions.</u> If you smile at a person and they break eye contact and do not smile back, then this is a negative. If you smile and nod and they look in the opposite direction, this is a negative. If you wave or point at them and they give you a look in disgust or sneer at you and then look away, then this is also a negative reaction.

- <u>Neutral reactions.</u> This is more of a non-reaction than a reaction. This type of non-reaction can often be misconstrued as a negative, but I assure you it is not. People that give you a neutral reaction are not necessarily unapproachable, but they will take an increased level of work if you wish to approach them.

If you smile at a person and they do not smile back at you, but they also do not break eye contact and continue to stare back at you, then this is a neutral reaction. If you smile and nod and they do not smile or nod, but they keep direct eye contact back with you, this also is a neutral reaction. The same goes with a point or a wave. If they don't respond with the same motion, but they also don't look away, then you can bet it's a neutral reaction.

Picking up on these simple little signs is an easy way to tell if someone is worth approaching or not and it takes a lot of guess work out of the whole process. This can also save you some embarrassment from thinking someone may be into you but actually isn't. Before I knew how to read these signs, I would tend to be frustrated and confused and rarely tried to go out of my way to talk to someone in fear of failure or embarrassment.

One time I was out with some friends at a Halloween function with about 500 people in attendance. We had been there for a couple of hours and I had seen quite a few attractive females by this time, so I thought it was time to try and talk with one. I picked out one girl that just happened to be in a VIP area with her girlfriends. Once I had rustled up enough courage, I walked over there and tried to talk with her. I was standing on the other side of the red tape for the VIP area and kind of half confidently asked her how she got into the VIP area. She looked at me like I was a peon and then and said, "What?" So I started to repeat myself by asking her how she got in there (I know, great pickup line right?). Before I could even finish what I was saying she literally put her hand up in front of me and physically pushed my face away in front of all her friends, my friends that were watching in anticipation, and all the other people that happened to be watching at the time.

I had never been more embarrassed in my life and I literally walked away and didn't attempt to talk to a girl for the rest of the night. To be honest, I didn't try talking to another girl for quite a long time after that. My confidence had literally been shot and destroyed. Now we can probably all agree that this girl was just a bitch and didn't need to respond the way that she did and was completely full of herself, which she was, and most likely had her own issues or reasons for being that way. But since that major embarrassment I vowed to myself that something like that would never happen again.

From that point on I decided to research as much as I could about male and female interactions and figure out how women thought towards men. I read books, went online, listened to webinars and spoke with people that knew more than I did. I became completely fascinated with the subject. Not only did I learn about how women thought, I also learned about how men thought as well, and how different men and women can be. It truly enhanced not only my life in general, but also my level of confidence.

So how could I be upset at some girl at a Halloween event when her actions towards me made such an impact? I took something negative and made it into a positive in my life, so really, I should be thanking this girl, whoever she is. I should also mention that since then I have never had such a negative experience in my life when trying to speak with someone. You see, to her, I was probably just a typical guy who posed a threat. If I try to think of it from her point of view, she may have had several negative experiences of her own which led her up to acting that way.

If I was a good-looking woman and had a bunch of condescending, half-confident men hitting on me all night with a bunch of cheesy pick-up lines when I was just trying to have a good time with my girlfriends, maybe I would be sick of it too, especially when I gave him absolutely no indication that I was interested in him. I still wouldn't reject a person in the way that she did, just because I think that's completely rude and I'm a nicer person than that, but I still don't blame her for being upset and reacting negatively.

Being able to read people's non-verbal communications and put myself in the position of the opposite sex has enabled me to make more informed decisions, therefore giving myself confidence in my actions. The same goes for anyone else, regardless if you're a man or a woman or a person of the same sex. You need to know what signals to look for and what signals to give if you see someone of interest or non-interest is looking at you. When you get to the point of actual verbal communication, it will decide whether the person likes you or not by how that communication is delivered, but at least you know you're not

going to get told off or embarrassed by someone reacting negatively

towards you. Worst case scenario is you have a conversation or

exchange a few words and move on.

CHAPTER 12: COMMUNICATING YOUR QUALITIES

All right, you've found someone you like and it appears that they are open to meeting you, so you want to walk over and start some verbal communication with them. This is where you've gotten past the physical test and you're going to need to prove that you can hold a conversation while holding their interest. How this part of communicating goes will determine whether this person will become interested in you or not, so it's good to have an idea of what you're doing.

If they've already given you a positive sign, then they are most likely attracted to you or you've drawn their curiosity in some way. A lot of people freeze and don't know what to say to start the conversation, or they think they need a witty pick up line to get the ball rolling or catch their attention or to make themselves stand out. This is completely unnecessary. Remember, if they gave you a positive reaction, then you already have their attention, so spouting off some cheesy pick up line will only turn them off.

STARTING THE CONVERSATION The simplest way to start a conversation is just to say a simple "Hello" and ask them how they are doing. Just make sure that you are being sincere. Keep eye contact and make sure that you have a smile on your face while you're doing it.

Smiling is a simple way to show that you are happy, and chances are that they won't be able to hold off on smiling back at you. The more that you walk around smiling, the more that people will wonder what you're happy about. It also helps you stand out in a positive way from those that aren't. Also, when you physically smile, it helps you become happier. Even if I'm in kind of a crappy mood, I just smile anyway, and before I know it I'm feeling happy again.

Now that you've said a quick hello and asked how they're doing or how their day is going, you will be able to read their reaction and judge just how open they are to you. This will coincide with their non-verbal reaction and whether it was a positive or a neutral. As I said earlier, if it was a neutral, then this person will most likely take a bit more work than a person who reacted with a positive.

If they were a neutral, then they will probably just say, "Hi" and give you a straight answer to your question. "Hi, I'm fine, thanks." They are going to make you work for it or prove to them why they should want to talk to you or even give you the time of day, whereas the person that gave you the positive will most likely answer your question and reply with a question of their own to keep the conversation going. "Hey! I'm good thanks. How's your day been so far?" It's obvious that the person that gave you the positive will be a lot easier to get to know than the neutral and will take a lot less work, so make sure if you're approaching a neutral that you think it's worth it and have something extra in your back pocket if you plan to go talk to them.

If you're speaking with a person that gave you a positive, then the conversation will probably just go along on its own and you probably won't need much advice on what to say, but it's always good to have a more than just a simple "Hello" ready when you go over there regardless. The best thing you can do is notice something about them or something that they are doing at that moment. Be observant of the situation and try to pick out something unique, especially if you're going to talk with someone that gave you a neutral.

It also helps to think of what you might want someone to say to you if they were to come over and try talking with you. If you're in a grocery store, be observant of what they have in their shopping cart or basket. Maybe they have an item in there that you really like and you can make a comment on it. For example, maybe they have a red Thai curry sauce and you can tell them that you love that type of Thai curry and that maybe you like making ethnic foods, followed up by asking them if they like cooking ethnic foods too. Then next thing you know, you're talking about cooking, which not only shows your interest, but it also shows that you have a skill. Showing that you have a skill will elevate your value and maybe it will open the door for them to ask what other skills you have or what other things that you like.

If you ever get stuck and don't know what to say, just try to keep asking questions. This will give you time to think of something to say back, or their response to your question may trigger a thought for you. It also gives you a way to steer the conversation in the direction that you want it to. As I mentioned in Chapter 4, the person who is asking the questions is the person controlling the conversation. It shows you're interested in them, but it also lets you get to know more about them.

KEEP EYE CONTACT Maintaining eye contact is a very crucial step to having a successful conversation. If you aren't keeping eye contact, not only does it show a lack of confidence, but it also shows a lack of interest. Also, if you don't have eye contact with the other person, it's quite likely that they will lose interest in you quickly or become distracted themselves. They will especially become distracted if you are in a bar type setting where there are lots of other people and they could be scanning around for their friends instead of listening to what you have to say.

Eyes can also be extremely seductive and show a lot about a person. If you're looking them in the eyes and not looking over them or around them or constantly in another direction, it shows that you're not a vain person and have a genuine interest in talking to them and getting to know them. It also can give the impression of honesty. Someone who can't look a person in the eyes will appear to have something to hide or a reason not to look at people directly

I was driving down a moderately busy street on a sunny day once and I noticed an attractive l girl driving the car beside me. Because it was a bright day, we both had our sunglasses on. When I looked over at her, she looked back at me. I immediately gave her a big smile and she immediately smiled back at me. I knew that I had a positive reaction from her, even without eye contact, because of how quickly she smiled back.

Because of the traffic, we got separated a bit, but the next time she was pulling up next to me I made sure that I had my sunglasses off and I looked right at her. To my surprise, she had removed her sunglasses as well and we made direct eye contact with one another. We both instantly started laughing in our cars. I gave her a nod and pointed at the next street ahead, with a motion for her to follow me. She changed lanes behind me and I pulled over on the next street. I had a quick hello with her and drove off two minutes later with her name and phone number and plans to meet up for a drink in the next couple of days.

When I drove off I started to think about what had just happened. I knew that eye contact was important, but at that point I also realized the power of it. Yes, we both smiled at one another and gave each other a positive, but it was the power of the eye contact that sealed the deal for us and made her physically take the action of pulling over and giving me her number.

ADJUST YOUR TONE Not just what you say, but how you say it will make an impression on someone you're speaking with. Your location and your environment will mainly determine what tone you need to use. If you're in a loud place like a bar or a noisy restaurant and you are forced to raise your voice, you will likely annoy the person and appear to be yelling, which will probably put the person off from you.

If you're in a quiet place and you're speaking too softly, that will show that you're unconfident and possibly uninteresting. You want to choose the correct tone not to turn the person off from you, but to also to help attract them to you. How you speak to a person can be just as sexy as how you're dressed or the way that you're looking at them.

When you're in a loud environment, you need a way to communicate so that they can hear you and you aren't yelling at them. At the same time, if there's loud music playing and they can't hear what you're saying, it will annoy them to keep having to ask what you said. The best way to deal with this situation is to reduce the space between yourself and them. This is a good opportunity to get a bit closer with someone and not have to worry about coming across as being creepy.

If it's loud enough, you may even want to be to the point where you are speaking with them cheek to cheek. Make sure that when you are doing this you aren't talking directly into their ear and that you are still back far enough that you can maintain eye contact. The closer you are to them, the more you will be able to continue reading their reactions. If you try to get a bit closer and they move away from you, then don't push it. Move back a bit. Once some time has passed, you can try going a bit closer again and see if they don't shy away this time.

Not only is tone about the volume of your voice, but it's also about the speed you're talking at and the way your voice comes across to the other person. If you're a woman and talk very quickly, you may come across as being a bubbly and high-strung person. If you're a man and talk very quickly, you might come across as being nervous and irritating. When you slow down your speech, not only will it be easier for the person you are speaking with to hear what you're saying, but it will also give you more time to think about what you're saying and what to say next.

Another good thing to do is to incorporate pauses between your sentences. This also will give you more time to think. Taking slight pauses can add sexual tension between you and cause arousal. Make sure when you're doing this that you keep looking at them and aren't looking away from them when you add pauses, or it will seem like you're trying to think of what to say.

Obviously, you don't want to speak too slowly either or you will just seem like you're slow in general. Find the right speed. Record yourself and play it back if you need to. This will give you a better idea of how you sound to others. Once you dial in the volume, tone and pauses, it will vastly improve your communication and ability to create a sexual tension between you and the person you're speaking with.

SEAL THE DEAL You don't really want your first communication to drag out or linger on more than necessary. You want to be somewhat brief and leave some mystery for them, so don't reveal too much. Unlike when you were practicing getting out of digital mode, this time you want to act like you're interested in them and finalize the deal.

Now this doesn't mean asking them back to your place right away. This isn't a book on how to be a pick-up artist and how to get someone in the sack as soon as possible. You've worked hard on yourself to make yourself high quality and high value, so you should expect the same from someone that you're interested in.

The best way to finalize the deal with someone and take things to the next level isn't just to ask them for their phone number. Give them an idea of something that you would like to do with them, but ask them in the form of a question. For example, you could ask, "What's your favorite drink?" Let's say they respond with, "I like martinis." Then you could say, "I know a place that makes great martinis. I'd love to take you there sometime." Make sure that you now ask them if they'd like to go there with you sometime. If they say yes, then you're good to go and now's also a good time to ask them for their name if you don't already know it.

When asking for their number don't just blurt out, "What's your phone number?" Be polite and ask them, "Would you mind if I had your number then?" Once they say yes, then get their number, or what I would do sometimes is just go to "add contacts" on my phone and simply hand it to them. This shows that you are also a trusting person, or if you are nervous and forget names, it also allows them to type in their own name, guaranteeing that you have the correct spelling.

If you ask the person to go out with you sometime and they seem hesitant, then they probably just need a little more reassurance, and that is totally fine. After all, they have just met you. If this occurs, then make sure you aren't being pushy or pressuring them. Make light of the situation. Say something funny to make them laugh. Call out the situation for what it is to help them feel comfortable. Say something like," What? You don't like dating complete strangers?" Once you make them laugh a bit and lighten the situation, they should start feeling a bit more comfortable and will most likely be okay with giving you their number.

DON'T TAKE IT PERSONALLY If it turns out that the person was willing to meet you and talk to you, but doesn't want to go on a date with you, then you need to be okay with it. Don't take this as a form of rejection and don't take it personally. You have no idea what's going on in this person's life. They could have just gone through a major breakup themselves and aren't ready to go on a date with someone yet.

Maybe the timing just isn't right for them or who knows, they may already be dating someone. Maybe they are leaving for a big trip in a couple of days or they are getting a transfer at work and there's no point in getting to know someone if they are just leaving anyway. And if it was because they just weren't into you, then you need to be okay with that too. It's better that you don't waste each other's time.

The best thing that you can do with someone that won't agree to a date with you is to not let it faze you. Keep a smile on your face and tell them it was nice to meet them. Don't act like it bothers you in even the slightest way. A lot of times they will regret not saying yes later down the road. They will appreciate how respectful you are and even wonder how you're so confident that you don't let it bother you. They may even change their answer just because of how well you handled them turning down a date. Being graceful, charming, and respectful goes a very long way with people.

CHAPTER 13: HANDLING THE DATE

Whether you're meeting someone you've met only online or someone you've briefly met in person, going on your first date with them can be a bit nerve racking, especially if it's something that you aren't used to. Of course, the more dates you go on, the more comfortable and confident you will feel. Meeting someone in a one-on-one situation will make you feel like you're on the spot to perform, which to a certain extent you are, but a one-on-one situation can also be very beneficial and in your favor.

Perhaps you met this person already and had to get their phone number in front of a group of their friends. Or maybe you met them online, but they probably had their friends look at your profile to get their opinion of you. Now you're in the situation where you are more in control of how things go, and if you act appropriately, you have a much better chance without any outside interference. Use this time when you're alone with them to your advantage by showing them your best side.

If they've already agreed to go on a date with you and they've shown up, then you know that they are attracted and interested in getting to know you. How the date goes will determine whether they agree to see you again or not. Up to this point, at least you know they like you so far, so you should it going. One of the best ways to do this is to create an aura for yourself.

WHAT IS AN AURA? An aura will help to ensure that someone forms an attraction for you and in some cases even an infatuation. An aura is difficult to explain . Some people refer to it as an energy that you project that other people around you can pick up on, and in some ways, it is. It sounds like a voodoo thing and may be hard to believe, but it's also something that's hard to deny. If you can give off an energy that attracts other people around you, then you will understand its importance when trying to attract someone.

Put it this way, have you ever been sitting at a traffic light and had a weird suspicion that someone is staring at you, and then you look over and someone is staring at you? Sometimes you don't even have to look in that direction; you just know. There are lots of women that have walked by a guy and just know that's he's staring at their ass as they walk away. They've probably even felt his eyes practically burning a hole in their ass from looking so hard. And then they look back and, BAM! He's staring right at it! Or how about if you go to work, and you can just tell one of your coworkers is in a shitty mood?

They can do their best to hide it physically and not show visible signs, but you can still pick up on it. And then you ask them what's bugging them and they let it out. They might even not tell you after asking them the first time and you almost need to force it out of them, but you knew it was there the whole time. This is also an example of feelings someone's energy. So now I'm sure you can agree that energy is out there and people can pick up on it.

CREATING AN AURA Everyone can project energy, but creating an aura is something much more complex. It takes conscious thought, knowledge, enthusiasm, humor, body language, self-animation, and most importantly, positivity. It takes a careful combination of these things to truly create an aura that people become subconsciously drawn to.

An aura is also something you don't want to mess around with if you're creating it with the wrong people. By that I mean that you may end up having someone drawn to you or become infatuated with you that you don't want to be that way with in return, so use it wisely. Infatuation can even grow into an unhealthy obsession as well, so be careful with it. Nobody wants to deal with a stalker. For obvious reasons, men won't have to worry as much, but women should be more careful with who they are trying to entice with a deep level of attraction and desire. That's not to say a woman can't become just as obsessive, but they won't pose the same physical threats that a man would to a woman.

There have been a few times where I did not realize I was creating an aura with the wrong women and have had to deal with the repercussions. A lot of times when someone is deeply drawn to you, it can be difficult for them to accept that you don't wish to become further romantic with them or be involved with them in a relationship at a deeper level than you already are. I've had women not be able to accept this, and I've even asked them, "Why me? I'm just a regular guy." Then when they try to answer it, they have difficulties and say things like, "I don't know. There's just something different about you," or "We just have so much fun together."

There are many people out there that understand the theories behind creating auras and use terms for them like "stealth attraction." This is where someone becomes deeply attracted to you in a subconscious manner without even knowing how or why they are so attracted to you. Many so-called males pickup artists use this as tactic to lure women into bed with them. When it comes down to it, no matter what you want to call it, creating an aura isn't a special power or magic. It's attaining, representing, and displaying certain qualities that people enjoy being around and feel good being around. Whenever you are speaking with someone, ask yourself, "Is this something that I would be attracted to or turned off by?" With that being said, let's look at what some of those things are and what it will take to build your own personal aura.

THE POWER OF POSITIVITY

As I said earlier, positivity is the most important thing when creating an aura for yourself. To recap, anyone can give off energy, but it takes something else to create an aura. That's because the energy that you project <u>must</u> be in the form of a positive energy. No one is going to be attracted to someone who constantly gives off negativity, but everyone enjoys being around someone who is naturally positive all the time.

Being able to see the positive in everything has helped me in my personal life as well as in my professional life. It's helped me problem solve through complicated situations to make the best of them, and it's helped me with many conflict resolutions between people to strengthen relationships and even friendships. Positivity is truly a powerful tool in your everyday life, so try to incorporate it as much as you can. The more positivity you put into your life, the more positivity will come out of your life as a result. You have the power to literally mold your life and shape it the way that you want with a consistent positive mindset.

If you aren't generally a positive person, then you will need to be aware of that and consciously work on it. Ask your closest friend(s) if they find you generally to be a mostly positive person or mostly negative person. Tell them you're working on yourself and would appreciate their honesty and would like them to be straight up with their response. If your best friend thinks you are negative more often than positive, then you've got some work to do. Don't be in denial. Own it and fix it.

Being positive always relates to being happy. If you are constantly being beaten down in life, then it can be hard to be positive all the time. Believe me. I know. My divorce was extremely rough on me, and as well I used to be a generally negative person in the past. I didn't realize that I clung to the bad in most situations and I had to become conscious of it. I asked a couple of my closest friends whether I came across being negative most of the time. They had trouble being direct with me at first, but I could tell what they thought by the looks on their faces. Eventually they let me know that I was a bit negative, in the nicest way possible of course. Once I was aware of this, I knew I had to change it. I didn't want to be known as that negative person that no one enjoyed being around.

People are literally drawn to positivity. Being positive is not a trick or ploy; it's an excellent quality to have. Part of my job as a manager was to hire and fire employees. I did most all the interviewing for my department, where I was forced to learn new skills of what to look for in people that would benefit the company.

What I started to learn was that I was hiring based on attitude more than on skills and experience. Of course, I needed people with experience, but if they had a poor attitude, they would be useless to me and create more problems than benefits. Someone with a great attitude and a positive mindset and a willingness to learn is far superior than someone who thinks they have put their time in and have a sense of self-entitlement.

I also found that negativity spreads much faster than positivity. If you have a group of people with positive attitudes and add a single negative person to that group, the negativity can spread to the others almost like a cancer. Before you know it, everyone is feeling negative and no one is happy with their job.

On the other hand, if you have a group that is entirely positive, or there is someone in the group that is truly powerfully positive enough to put the negative person in their place, the group becomes extremely happy about their jobs and accomplishments, thus becoming more productive and easier to deal with. As a manager, would you rather have a group of individuals working for you that is negative or positive? Positive of course. Well, the same goes for people that you are on a date with. You can be the best-looking person in the room, but if you're constantly negative, you will very quickly become the most unattractive one in the room.

ENTHUSIASM

Being enthusiastic is a form of showing physical energy and interest in your conversation with someone. If you're enthusiastic, it generally means that you are happy and engaged in what the other person is saying. If you're enthusiastic about something you're telling them, then it also shows them that you are passionate about what you're talking about. If you can be animated about something that's going on in your life, then it also expresses to the person that you might one day can be passionate about them or a relationship with them.

Being enthusiastic is great, but don't be overenthusiastic either. You must be genuine with your excitement or you will come across as being fake or bubbly. Be conscious of your attitude and be sincere with it. You don't want to annoy the person, the same as you wouldn't want to annoy them with the tone of your voice.

People appreciate enthusiasm and usually it becomes contagious and easy for the other person to feel the same way. Highly motivated people are usually enthusiastic people as well. They motivate themselves to become excited about themselves and whatever they want to accomplish, and this leads them to raise their energy levels. Genuine enthusiasm partnered with positivity is a great way to start creating an unmistakable aura around yourself.

LISTEN

Attentively listening to someone and being engaged in what someone is saying shows that you care and are interested in what they are saying. Sometimes when you get caught up too much in the dating game, things can get repetitive. After a while, you can even start to mix up stories or get things confused. This is a great way to make someone feel unimportant and will hinder you from having an aura.

Now, I'm not perfect. I've done this before, but I've also had it done to me, and I know how it made me feel, so I understand it. I'm sure we've all had that one friend that is a horrible listener, and it makes you feel like he or she just doesn't give a shit. You listen to their stories all the time, and then when you start to tell them something, they are looking around the room or on their phone or not paying attention. It makes you not want to share yourself with that person or tell them any kind of personal information about yourself.

Giving a person your full attention shows them respect and makes them feel important rather than frustrated and unimportant. You want this person to share their thoughts with you. When you become truly engaged in a conversation with someone, they will tend to want to communicate more with you. The more they talk to you, the more you will know about them. The more you know about them, the more they will trust you. Do not take advantage of their trust. This is the start of how lifelong friendships are formed. If a person feels comfortable opening up to you and knows that you are listening to what they are saying, they will sometimes tell you things that they haven't told anyone, not even friends that they have had for years.

MAKE THEM FEEL GOOD

Have you ever had a conversation with someone that made you feel good about yourself? Hopefully everyone has, because it's an awesome feeling to experience. When you make someone feel good about themselves, it also makes them feel good to be around you. They will associate their happiness and feeling good about themselves with being around you.

For example, if someone is telling you they just got a promotion at work, then tell them they totally deserved it because of how smart they are. Tell them about a quality that you see in them. Even if they tell you they didn't get a promotion that they wanted, you could say something like, "What's wrong with the people at your work? Don't they know how smart you are? You totally deserve it." Not only does that make them feel good about themselves, but it also makes them feel good about being around you, even if they are telling you a bad piece of news. A simple comment like that can change a person's entire day.

Be careful not to overdo this either. Again, you need to be genuine with everything that you say, the same as you would want other people to be genuine with what they are telling you. Otherwise, it's completely meaningless. Practice this with your friends or people at your work if you need to. You can watch their moods elevate and usually even see physical signs of appreciation, like a smile or a touch on the arm.

BE MODEST

The last thing that you want to do when you are on a date with someone is to start bragging about yourself. Bragging is probably one of the worst turnoffs that a person can do, and modesty will go a lot further for you. Nobody wants to sit at a table and listen to people talk about themselves the entire time. Bragging also shows insecurity and makes it appear that you are conceited, vain, and trying to prove your worth as a person.

If you have a nice car or a nice house or an awesome job, then keep it to yourself. Don't offer any of this information unless they ask you. Even when they do ask you, don't answer the question easily, and make it seem like it's not important to you. If you do have some nice things this will be an asset for you as it shows that you are physically capable of earning money and therefore able to look after a potential child or family, but let them find out about these things on their own.

If you both share a common interest like European sports cars and are talking about your favorite cars for part of your date and you own a nice European sports car, then don't tell them. Keep it to yourself. Then when you're leaving and they see you get into your

Mercedes AMG and drive off, that will instantly elevate your value and attractiveness. If you were to tell them about it, then seeing you get into your sports car will lose its effectiveness. Let them find out these things on their own.

USE YOUR HUMOR

Using some humor in your conversation helps open people up and gives you a chance to get to know someone better. I'm sure you've heard the expression "breaking them out of their shell." Well, humor has a great way of doing that. Also, humor can be an attractive feature to have. People seem to be more attracted to someone with a good sense of humor over someone who is a straight edge and doesn't crack a smile.

Have you ever told a joke to someone and they just didn't get it? Or maybe it just didn't seem funny to them at all, even though it was completely hilarious to you. Then you tell that very same joke to someone else and they find it just as comical as you do. Doesn't it make you feel a lot better when you tell that joke to the person that gets it? Sometimes you just need to break yourself out of your own shell and stop taking life so seriously. Humor also shows that you are happy and present in the moment. Humor can be magnetic, so try to bring out your sense of humor.

BE ANIMATED

Don't be afraid to show your expression in the physical form when you're having a conversation with someone. Everyone knows that Italians tend to wave their hands around in the air when they are talking as a way of being animated and showing expression. Some Italians might even need to tone the arm waving down a bit, and you don't want to overdo it either. Some people might find it embarrassing to sit next to someone that looks like they are conducting an orchestra or guiding a Being 747 down a runway, so try to find a happy medium.

Being animated can create a unique experience with someone and can be somewhat fascinating. Being enthusiastic also shows a level of engagement and passion in the conversation. Using animated movements while talking with someone creates a different experience over the usual type of conversation where a person is just sitting and not moving. It almost brings a physical presence to a mere verbal conversation. Being animated means showing signs of expression in your facial movements, arm movements, hand movements, and if you're a woman then you're lucky enough to be able to use hair movements.

A simple toss of the hair from a woman can be very attractive to a man. Hair can be one of the sexiest parts of a woman, so if you have long hair then use it to your advantage. Men also find the neck area sexy, so try sliding your hand through your hair and curling your hair up over your ear to expose your neck. If you see his eyes watching your neck, then you know it's working.

If you're a man and see a woman playing with her hair quite a bit, then pick up on the sign, because she's being flirtatious with you. A toss of the hair from a woman can also send him a waft of her scent. He might smell her perfume or conditioner, something that can create an instant memory for him. Smell is the number one trigger and the most powerful sense that is directly related to memory.

BE KNOWLEDGEABLE

Being knowledgeable is a great asset to have. When you show general knowledge, it displays intelligence and participation. If you have a good general knowledge of basic world news and what's going on around you, it can elevate your attractiveness and cause people to look at you in an envious fashion.

No one is saying you need to be a political leader or anything, but if you're just one of those people that seem to always have a good grasp on what's going on in the world, that will play a beneficial role in creating yourself an aura. People look up to other people that seem to know more about everyday life than they do, or if they do have a good grasp of the world around them, they will appreciate your being able to keep up with them.

If you can combine these qualities, you will have no problems creating an aura that will draw others towards you and make them want to be around you as much as they can. It's difficult to combine these things all the time, but the more you are aware of them and actively practice them, the easier it will become. So, remember to be positive, enthusiastic, listen, make them feel good, be modest, use your humor, be animated, and be knowledgeable.

DON'T TALK ABOUT YOUR EX If it hasn't been that long since the breakup, you might still have the tendency to bring up your ex occasionally. Do yourself a favor and save the ex-talk for when you're with your friends, family or counsellor. Sometimes when you are dating someone who wants to know more about you, you can mention that you're out of a long-term relationship, but don't talk about specifics. If the two of you end up becoming more serious, then it might be appropriate to tell them more about you and your ex several dates down the road, but for now stay away from story-telling and being specific.

To use an analogy, think about it as if you were to be selling your house. If you have a good real estate agent, they will tell you to take down all your family photos and anything else that may be personal. The reason for this is to allow the potential buyer to visualize themselves living in the home. If you have a lot of family photos up, they won't be able to see themselves living there. The same goes for when you're on a date with a potential partner. You want them to allow themselves to visualize being in your life and that will be more difficult if you keep mentioning personal stories and experiences with your ex-partner.

When the time is right, the other person will probably inquire and want to know more about your ex. When this happens, it is very important, regardless of what happened, <u>not</u> to trash- talk your ex-partner. If you do talk poorly about your ex, the person will automatically be wondering "How can he talk so badly about someone that he used to love?" They will also think that you would be capable of talking about them that way if they were ever to get close with you. So try not to slander your ex when you're speaking with a new potential partner, or you could hinder yourself in the end.

Even if your ex was the worst person in the world and really made a mess of your life, continuing to feel anger or resentment shows that you aren't fully over that person and will throw up some red flags for any new prospects. Simply saying that you weren't meant to be with your ex and that things didn't work out is much more tactful, especially if you end up telling them the story of what actually happened. Then they would be thinking, "Wow, they went through a lot with their ex and they still don't talk down on them." This shows that you are in control of your emotions and that you've done a lot of work on yourself. It also shows that you can commit to working on yourself to take corrective actions in your life.

CREATING SEXUAL TENSION Creating sexual tension is a great way to heat things up, but also, it's a way of keeping out of the oh-so-famous "friend zone." We've already discussed how slowing your speech, using the right tone, and incorporating pauses can create a sexual tension, but there are also other ways to spice up the chemistry between you and your date.

Look at Her Lips. If you're a man, then take note of what makes a woman sexy. No, I don't mean her breasts and butt. Women use make up to enhance features that attract men and increase their sexuality and femininity. For example, they wear lipstick to amplify the sexuality of their lips. A woman's lips can be very sexy, and a great way for a man to create a sexual tension is to notice them on a woman. I don't mean to sit there and stare at her lips all night.

We already know that we must keep eye contact to keep interest, but if you take slight moments to look down and notice how sexy her lips are and go right back to eye contact she will notice that you have looked at her lips. Only do this for a brief second and at a quick glance. She might not notice the first time you do this, but after a couple of times, she will take notice. She might say something or she might not, but she will notice.

If she asks if you were staring at her lips, then admit it and don't hide it. Apologize and tell her that she has nice lips. Most likely, she will thank you for the compliment, but what this will also do is show her is that it wasn't just something meaningless that you told her. If a guy meets a girl and tells her that she has beautiful eyes, then she will be flattered. At the same time, it might be something he tells all the girls that he meets and can come across as a bit meaningless.

If you're having a conversation with a woman and you don't say anything about her lips, but she catches you noticing them, then it tells her you find her lips sexy and couldn't help but keep looking at them while trying not to get caught. This has much more depth behind it and creates a greater sexual chemistry because she knows you find something sexy about her.

Biting your Lower Lip. If you're a woman, then your lips can be very sexually appealing to a man. Wear a lipstick that accents your lips and shows how sexy they are. When you add a gloss to your lips it also helps them stand out and adds a level of sex appeal to them for a man. A man will always notice women's lips, so use this to your advantage. When you slightly bite your bottom lip from time to time, it's a way of flirting with him and can inject a sexual appeal into your conversation. Of course, you don't want to overdo this, so use your common sense and discretion for when and how often you do this.

Lingering Touches. Breaking the physical barrier is a good way to explore how well your date is going. When you're talking to your date, try a slight touch to their forearm and see how they react. If they pull away from you, then wait awhile before trying this again. If you add a touch again and they are receptive and do not pull away, then things are going fine.

To increase the sexual tension try leaving your hand there a bit longer than you normally would. Adding this lingering touch can be arousing to the other person and help take your date to the next level. If they are receptive and don't pull away, then you may even find that they reciprocate by touching you back. From here you can increase the sexual chemistry even further by touching their leg or hand. Just be careful not to overdo things too quickly.

Sexual Compliments. As we discussed earlier, complimenting someone makes them feel good about themselves. Adding a sexual component to this makes people feel good about themselves at an attractive level. I don't mean that you should just tell them that you think they're hot. This will just make you come across as being shallow. Pick something out about them that you find attractive and try to incorporate this in your conversation when the timing is right.

If you're a woman and find that your date has nice arms and you're talking about something that involves lifting you could say, "I'm sure you don't have problems lifting anything with arms like that." If you're a man and find your date's legs attractive and you're talking about dating, you could say something like, "I'm sure you have no problems meeting men with legs like that." When you pick out specific things that you find sexy about them, it shows that you find them attractive and have noticed something specific about them. They will be flattered, but at the same time you're adding a level of physical sexuality to your conversation.

Be Playful. Being playful is also a way of flirting with your date. A great way to be playful is with laughs and smiles, but also with eye contact. If your date is looking away at something, you can keep looking right at them, and then when they look back in your direction, quickly glance away and pretend that you weren't staring at them. Then look back at them, keeping a playful grin on your face. Having playful eye contact also shows that you aren't just interested in being their friend and will encourage them to be playful back with you.

CHAPTER 14: WHERE TO FIND A POTENTIAL PARTNER

The first thing to decide on when you're looking for a potential partner is to figure out what kind of relationship you want. If you're still fresh out of your relationship when you finish reading this book, you probably aren't going to want to jump straight into another relationship. You're more likely to be looking for a short-term relationship with the possibility of it opening into something else. If you've been dating for a while now and you know what you're looking for and feel that you've completed a good portion of the healing process, then you're probably going to be looking for a long-term relationship.

Whichever kind of relationship you're looking for, it's important to be honest with yourself. If you don't want to get into anything serious but you still want to meet people, go on dates and have casual sex. That's okay. Humans are meant to have physical interactions with one another, and there's nothing wrong with that. The important thing is to be honest with yourself and to give yourself what you need.

SHORT-TERM DATING When you're getting back out into the dating world short-term dating can be a lot of fun, and you will likely meet a lot of new people and make new connections. When you do connect with someone and the result is casual sex, you can sometimes have feelings of guilt in the beginning, as if you were doing something wrong. This is a natural feeling to have, and it will eventually recede. Because you were in a long-term relationship prior to dating, it's normal to feel this way and understandable that you would feel like you're doing something wrong.

Not only is it important for you to be honest with yourself about short-term dating, it's also important to be honest with the people that you are dating. You don't want to be someone that goes around having sex and lying to a bunch of people. This will only hurt the people around you and eventually it will catch up with you and you will be hurt yourself. It won't feel good to the people you do this to, and you won't feel good about yourself if you do this.

If you're into short-term dating, then you need to go where other people that are into that type of dating will be. Short-term dating is mostly associated with night life, but that's not to say that you can't meet people during the day as well. It's also not to say that just because you have short-term dating goals that you can't end up meeting the right person and having a long-term relationship with them, so be open to that as well. All it takes is meeting the right person.

Typical places to meet people for short-term dating are by going where there is a larger selection than other places. You would want to go where your odds are in your favor. If you're a man, you should consider going where there are typically more women than men, and if you're a woman you would want to go where there are typically more men. If you're still young, then you will be more inclined to go to places that have a good night life, like a night club, dance club or popular bar. The odds are usually even, but try to go where there are typically more of the people of sex that you prefer. If you're gay, then obviously you are going to go to a place where there are typically other gay people to increase your odds.

If you're not into the whole night club type scene, then I suggest going to places that are a little more laid back that you will enjoy, like a jazz bar or maybe a place with a lounge type of atmosphere. Look online and try to find somewhere that has fancy cocktails or is a little classier. It's also a good idea to go somewhere that isn't quite as noisy, where it could be easier to have a conversation with someone. There's nothing wrong with going to a social house and having a meal at the bar, even if you're on your own, and especially if there's a good sports game on.

If you're a woman and sitting on your own watching a game at the bar, trust me that it won't be long before a man wants to talk with you, regardless of where you sit. If you're a guy, then pay attention to where you take a seat. If there's a bunch of guys on one end of the bar and a woman on her own at the other end, then sit at the end with the woman. Don't sit right next to her, so you don't intimidate her or appear to be a threat, but sit a couple of seats away.

Even if there isn't a woman sitting at the end on her own, always take a seat where you can be as open as possible and away from the other men. Also, try not to sit at the end where there is an open seat on only one side of you. Increase your odds by having a seat on either side of you and if the place gets busy a woman might have no choice but to sit next to you. It's always a good idea to strike up a conversation with the bartender.

Whether it's a male or female bartender doesn't matter. Bartenders are used to conversations with people, and talking with them will get your social juices flowing. Because you don't want to be the type of person who just sits and stares at the screen the whole time and doesn't say a word to anyone, speaking with the bartender will help to elevate your value.

LONG-TERM DATING The best advice that I can give someone who is looking for a long-term partner is not to look at all. That advice may seem crazy to a lot of people, but I truly believe that this is the best way to meet a potential lifelong partner. If you are trying to attract a person you want to spend the rest of your life with, then it's important to meet someone who has common interests with you. Some of the best places to meet someone with interests similar to yours are places where you like to be. Hopefully that isn't sitting at home on the couch watching TV; otherwise you will have a hard time meeting anyone at all. What I mean is get out there and enjoy the activities that you like to participate in.

If you don't have a lot of hobbies and interests, then try to get some new ones and experience life. If you are the type of person that like to stay physically active, then think about joining a cross-fit class or maybe a yoga class. If you're into sports, then try joining a local sports team. Joining a team sport like softball or soccer is not only a great opportunity to meet someone with similar interests, but it's also a good way to make friends. The more friends you have, the more your friendship tree will branch out, and the more people and opportunities you will be exposed to.

When you just go and enjoy the things that make you happy in life, it's more likely that the right person will eventually come to you than if you were to go out and constantly hunt for them. It's also a much more natural way to meet someone. The more you become the person that you want to meet, the more you will attract those types of people into your life.

ONLINE DATING When you are online dating, it's important to know the basics of how to attract the type of potential partner that you want. The great thing about online dating is that you can set your preferences to whatever you desire. If you're just looking for casual sex, then you can set your preference to that category and eliminate anyone looking for a serious relationship. If you're looking for a serious relationship, you can set your preference and eliminate people who are looking only for casual sex.

After you have chosen your dating preference, it's important to create a profile to display your best attributes, and it's also important to display them in the right way. When you're choosing your photos, you obviously want to select pictures where you look your best, but you also don't want to choose photos that make you look conceited or vain. That means keeping the mirror selfies to yourself. If you're a guy, you don't want to use the typical shirtless mirror selfie. If you're a woman, although you can get away with a lot more selfies than a man, you want to keep the typical duck face selfies to a minimum.

Your profile picture should be one of you that clearly has a visible shot of your face. That can be difficult to do without taking a selfie, but try to use a photo that isn't, or have a friend take one for you. Your other photos should show your talent or skills. If you like watersports, then use a pic that shows you doing watersports. If you participate in yoga, then include a photo of you practicing yoga, and again try to have a friend take it for you. Other photos should show you with friends and/or family. Use photos where you look happy and show that you have good social abilities and friendships. Illustrating that you have social status is also another way of elevating your value and displaying that you can have relationships, even if it's with friends or family members.

When creating your write-up. try to avoid saying too much about yourself and your wants. Instead, try to tell about what you enjoy and the activities that you like to spend your time doing. If you write too much about what you're looking for in a man or a woman, you can scare off potential partners who don't fully meet your criteria. If you include more about what you enjoy and like to do, they will picture doing those things with you and fitting in instead.

Although you want to be honest, if you're just wanting casual sex, don't just say you are "DTF" or that all you want is to get laid. If you're a woman and write that, then you will no doubt get a flurry of men that will respond to you, but, trust me, they will not be of the caliber that you are wanting. If you are a man and you write this (unless you're gorgeous), even women who are wanting casual sex will keep looking right past you. And if you do get responses from women, they also will not be of the caliber that you are looking for. Many people who are only wanting casual sex still to want to be open to the opportunity and possibility of something greater coming from it.

HOW MEN AND WOMEN CAN DIFFER IN DATING GOALS

An important point to make is that even though you may set your preference to eliminate people looking for another preference, you may still get people who are not being honest with their preferences. For example, if you're a woman indicating serious relationship only. you might get men that show up as serious relationship even though they want casual sex.

The reason for this is that men and women differ in how they try to attract the opposite sex. Men sometimes act as if they are looking for a long-term relationship while they are really hoping for a short-term relationship with a woman, whereas women can sometimes act as if they only want a short-term relationship from a man to hopefully get a long-term relationship from him.

Men and women differ in this way because in the beginning of the relationship it's usually up to the woman to decide if she will have sex with the man. It's her turn to be selective and decide if she wants to sleep with him or not, so he will have to display his best attributes until she makes her decision. Once she makes the decision to sleep with the man, it then usually becomes the man's decision whether or not to continue the relationship with the woman. It's now his turn to be more selective, and it's up to the woman to show her worthiness as a long-term partner.

Whether it seems fair or not, this is just the natural course of action that usually takes place between men and women. Therefore, the opposite sex can sometimes fake a mating goal to achieve what they want. A man can fake wanting a long-term relationship to get casual sex, and a woman can fake wanting a short-term situation in hopes that he will want to keep pursuing the relationship after sex. This is also why men tend to be the ones to "fly the coop" after they've gotten into a woman's pants.

CHAPTER 15: LAW OF ATTRACTION

The law of attraction is something that can't be ignored, and if you don't know much about it then I suggest picking up the book "Law of Attraction" and reading about it. The main parts of the law of attraction that would relate to someone looking for a relationship are thinking about what type of person you want in your life and how you think of that person being in your life. The law of attraction is about how to achieve the things that you want in your life. If you want love in your life, then you need to picture having love in your life. Therefore, many people make vision boards so they can picture something in their life. This also goes for material items as well, like cars, houses, boats or whatever you want to obtain.

VISUALIZING YOUR PARTNER Think about what you want in your life as far as a partner. Think about what kind of person they would be and what qualities that you would want them to have. Do you want them to be outgoing or shy? Do you want them to be active and into sports, or would they be more of a person who wants to stay in and watch a movie? Would your perfect partner want to travel with you? Do you want them have family goals as far as having children, or would you rather they didn't?

Now picture what that person would look like. Would they be thin or have more of an athletic build? Maybe you prefer someone who is a bit curvy. Are they blonde, brunette or a redhead? Would they be tall or would they be short? The more detailed you become with visualizing the perfect person for you, the better. Think of the person that you think would be perfect for you and visualize them being in your life. Maybe they look slightly like your ex or maybe they are completely opposite.

Regardless of what type of person they would be, it's important to visualize them and see them as part of your life. The more you picture this person being in your life, the more you will become familiar with the idea of finding that person and having them enter your life. You also want to concentrate on the things that you already have, rather than the things that you don't.

Rather than thinking about the fact that you went through a major breakup and lost someone that was close to you, think about all the people that you do have in your life. Think about all of your family and friends. If you don't have a lot of friends, then think of all the friends that you will have after meeting new people.

HOW YOU PICTURE YOUR PARTNER It's not about just picturing your perfect partner, but it's also about how you picture your perfect partner. A lot of people go through life with a tendency to look at what they don't have rather than what they do have. They also tend to live for their future rather than their present. This is the way that most of us have trained ourselves because of how we are brought up in society.

We sometimes look at things in a negative way rather than positive. For example, someone who wants a new Porsche but drives an old Honda because they can't afford a sports car might concentrate on the fact they are driving an old Honda rather than focusing their energy on obtaining the new Porsche. They might think of it as, "I wish I made more money so that I could have a Porsche," or "Why can't I have a better job so that I can have a Porsche?"

It is quite common for most people to think this way, but to change our thoughts and focusses we literally need to retrain ourselves and our way of thinking. This is not as easy as it sounds at first, but after conscious efforts, we can develop a new way of thinking and attract the things that we want into our lives.

If you picture having a new Porsche in your life, then you can have a new Porsche and the power to do that is totally in your hands. Instead of looking at what you <u>don't</u> have, you need to shift your thoughts and think of it what you <u>can</u> have. An example of this would be, "I can't wait until I have a new Porsche" or "I can't wait until I make enough money to get a Porsche." This shifts your thoughts from focusing on what you don't have and retrains your brain into thinking about what you will have.

The brain is a very powerful tool and is very adaptable with how you develop it. If you truly want something in your life, then your brain will find a way to get it, no matter what you need to change in your life to obtain it. This also includes love, sex, relationships and people. If you truly want love in your life, then focus on having love again, rather than focusing on not having love. Instead of thinking "Why can't I find love?" or "When am I ever going to find love again?" shift your focus and try to think of it as "I can't wait until I find love again" or "I can't wait until I find the person that I'm going to fall in love with."

Incorporating the law of attraction into your life is another way of adding positivity to your life. Just as we discussed earlier, the more that we add positivity to our lives, the more positivity we will receive from our lives. Staying positive, using the law of attraction, and being consistent will increase your chances of finding love again.

CHAPTER 16: KNOWING IT'S THE ONE

Here's the question of all questions, "How do you know when you've met the one?" Unless you're an especially intuitive person, you might not know if you've met the one you're meant to spend the rest of your life with. I mean, let's face it, you've already been through a traumatic experience with someone that you thought was "the one." So what's different this time?

Well, intuition is something that can help you out with this, but there are also a lot of other factors that play a role on knowing if you've met the love of your life or not. After all, no one wants to make the same mistake twice - not just because you don't want to look silly but also because you don't want to put yourself or anyone else through that sort of pain and agony again.

There can be a lot of factors that can distract you from seeing who you're in a relationship with, mostly in the beginning when there are fireworks going off and you can't keep your hands off each other. When this stage starts to slow down a bit and you really get to know someone, you will get an idea of what they are really like as a person and in a relationship. I'm sure you're already aware of some red flags to watch out for from your past relationship, so you will be more intuitive with what kind of person you are dating.

What you want to be able to do is step outside of your relationship and look at it from a third person point of view and not as someone in the relationship. You may need to go somewhere and take some time to yourself to clear your mind. This may take a while, so don't beat yourself up if you can't clear your mind right away. Just give it some time and try not to think too much. This is more of a feeling exercise. This is another situation where you will need to trust what your guts are telling you.

When you finally manage to get to a place where you're relaxed with a clear mind and you can think from an outside perspective, then ask yourself some simple questions. How does that person treat you in the relationship? What does the big picture look like? Are they adding a positive impact to your life or implanting negativity? Does this person bring out the best in you or do you feel like you're just not yourself within the relationship? Is he or she supportive of you and everything you do in your life? Do they generally make you feel happy, or are you feeling anxious and stressed out?

These are all important questions to ask, and sometimes if you think of them just as two people and not yourself in the relationship, you will find it's easier to see the truth of the relationship so that you are not making excuses for the actions of the person you are with. Your gut feelings will tell you whether this feels like a good relationship or a bad one, and if your head is clear, it shouldn't be too difficult for you to come to this conclusion.

DON'T GET CAUGHT UP IN THEIR BEAUTY Now when I make the comment not to get caught up in their beauty, what I'm saying is not to get caught up in the exterior beauty. Sometimes it can be easier to overlook some of the negative things that someone is doing to you when you are very attracted to that person. Don't let the physical beauty of a person with a perfect body and face cover up what they are really like on the inside. The way to judge if a person is the right one for you or not is not to focus on their physical characteristics. This person could look exactly the way that you want them to, and they could be a very eloquent and poised talker when it comes to handling themselves in a conversation, but they may not be having a positive impact on your life.

Your family and friends all may have told you, "Wow, you sure scored a looker!" but if that person talks poorly to you or about you, people close to you aren't going to have nice things to say about them. It's the inner qualities that will help you decide whether this person is a good person.

ARE YOU COMFORTABLE TOGETHER? Usually when you meet someone, there is a level of comfort almost immediately, but sometimes this takes more time to build. Either way, you need to be comfortable with them at all times. When you're with them, does it feel like you're home? Or do you feel like a visitor in their house? There may be a lot of people you have met that you feel comfortable with, but with your life partner this should be a whole different extreme. You want to be able to feel not only comfortable, but you want to feel a high level of safety when you're with them.

Trust is something that will make you feel safe, so if you have a level of trust for one another, then a level of safety should accompany it as well. Think about it. If this is someone you want to spend the rest of your life with, then you should both feel especially comfortable around each other.

BEST FRIENDS Every life-long partner should not just feel like they are dating their friend, but they should still feel like best friends in a way. Of course, they aren't taking the place of your best friend, but you need to feel like you can do almost anything you would with your best friend without having to worry about it. It also helps if the two of you share some common hobbies or interests so t you can enjoy doing them together as friends.

You should be able to laugh with them and have them laugh with you just the same way you would with a best friend. When you think of doing something in your life, such as going on a vacation or traveling somewhere, you should think about wanting to do it with them being there as well. And this shouldn't be through familiarity. It should be through choice and you should want them there because they feel like your best friend.

TRUST THOSE THAT YOU SHOULD TRUST If you have best friends and family members that know you and what makes you tick, then you should trust their opinions to a certain degree. Ultimately when it comes down to it, it's your decision who you will spend your life with, but you should also consider what their opinions are. They will give you an outside perspective that will hopefully be unbiased. Obviously, you don't want to listen to the opinion of a friend that is constantly jealous of you, but if that's the case, why are they your friend?

You want to have a general vibe about what everyone's feelings are. Sometimes people won't tell you, but if you ask, chances are you will get a general feeling on everyone's thoughts. The opinions of people who know you best should help you confirm your own feelings.

Another thing your friends and family will help you with is seeing how your partner acts towards them. Are they kind and respectful to your friends and family? Or do they treat them poorly or with arrogance? How they treat the people that are important to you is a good indication of the type of person they are. If they respect you, they will be respectful towards your friends and family, even if they don't fully agree with who your friends are.

YOUR LEVEL OF EXCITEMENT Your level of excitement is also an indication of whether he or she is right for you. When your busy work day is over and you're on your way home, are they on your mind? If you're living together, are you crazy excited to see them when you get there? Maybe you're so excited that you can't wait, and you usually end up calling them on your drive home.

If you're excited about your partner all the time, this is a good indication that they could be the right one, but just like everything else in life, it must go both ways. This means that the other person needs to be enthusiastic and feel the same way about you in return. If it's only you getting excited and your partner never seems to show the same feeling towards you as you do for them, that's not a good sign. Maybe they are the type of person that just never gets excited about anything in life, but then you'd have to be willing to sacrifice that excitement, and that's a big sacrifice.

IT'S UP TO YOU As I said before, it's ultimately your decision on whether you feel this is the right person for you or not. These are merely tips and suggestions on ideas to help you make an informed decision for yourself. You are the only one who can truly know your feelings towards someone and how they make you feel. Being with someone wonderful will truly shine through.

It's not just about being with someone that makes you feel good about them, but it's also about how they make you feel about yourself that makes a difference. If you feel good about yourself being with them and they make you feel important and loved, then it sounds like you're on the right track and with the right person. Everyone has baggage in one form or another, but no one should be the baggage themselves. How they handle themselves around you and treat you, no matter what baggage they have, is what's important.

If we've gone through divorce or a major breakup, then we ourselves also have baggage and need to have patience occasionally, but that doesn't give us the right to treat others poorly. There's a saying I really like that goes "Let your past make you better, not bitter." These are useful words to live by, and hopefully you and your partner will follow them.

CHAPTER 17: KEEPING YOUR SUCCESS

Once you're lucky enough to find that one person that you feel is someone you want to spend your life with, it's important to know that your work isn't done yet. Oh no, it can't be that easy! You see, love is still a complicated thing, and if you wish to keep it, then you will always have to put in work.

The best way to keep love in your life is to work smarter and not harder. Of course, there are things you've learned in this book that will help you along the way, like being self-aware and sensitive to other people's emotions. But that's just the start of keeping lasting love. I recommend that you continue reading and doing research on what it takes to keep a good relationship. Taking these small steps will help you along with maintaining a healthy and enjoyable relationship.

I also, to this day, read up on what it takes to understand women better and how I can maintain a happy relationship. I recommend reading up on *The 5 Love Languages*. There are many tests you can take online that will show you ways that you can receive love from someone. Whether it's from receiving gifts to receiving quality time, you need to understand your own needs and the needs of your partner.

Your idea of how to feel loved could be completely opposite to your partner's idea of how to feel loved. This is a big mistake and a big miscommunication between many partners that can result in relationship failure. Men and women have many ways of misunderstanding each other, and this is a typical example of how, so learn about it and be on top of your game.

It's always good to use specific examples with your partner. For example, if your partner's love language is words of affirmation and you want to tell them they look handsome or pretty, don't just tell them they look good today. That can be taken as an insult. They may think "Well, how do I look on other days?" And then they can take it as a negative instead of a positive. Instead, try telling them that the outfit they are wearing looks so good on them and they are so fashionable with everything they wear. It will go a lot further as a compliment.

Just as we've discussed earlier in this book, many of the ways that men and women react and perceive each other are derived from prehistoric times. Times have changed greatly and so has the dating world. The more you know about the way they've changed, the better chances you'll have at keeping your successful relationship.

Back in the day, things were a lot simpler. Men went hunting and left the women at home in the cave to look after their home and children. The men only had one job: go get food and bring it back to the family. The women had to stay in the cave and tend to the children, and when the man came home with food, it was her job to tend to the man for risking his life to keep them fed. It was simple, but clearly more dangerous, and men had a lot more risk than they do now.

With the current situation of men and women both going to work and putting food on the table and coming home after a hard day of work it's important to know how this has changed things between the sexes. By being aware of these changes, you will find simple solutions that you may have not seen before. I highly recommend reading *Together Forever* by John Gray. He goes through the changes in communication and the small, simple steps it takes to give and receive the love that you and your partner are looking for.

As an example, from Gray's book, it's now important that a man listens to a woman and learns about her day first, before he with receives any kind of tending from the woman. Prehistorically, women had other women is society that they would create close relationships with just in case the man was killed while trying to find food. Then she would have protection provided by the other women in their society. Now when a woman comes home from work, she needs a man to listen to her in place of a woman in society. If she receives this, she will feel fulfilled and then tend to the man's needs.

The man doesn't need to and shouldn't try solving the woman's problems. She only needs to be listened to. A man's instinct is to try to solve problems. Example, if a car has squeaky brakes the man's instinct is to try to figure out what's wrong with them and fix them. Therefore, it can be difficult for a man not to interfere and only listen, but if the man tries to solve all her issues, he will only cause more issues.

With all the hard work that you've done to get over your divorce and find new love, it's worth it to put in that extra bit of work to keeping it. Understanding the opposite sex will go a long way not just for having a good relationship, but also for basic communication in your day-to-day life.

Divorce is a painful struggle that many underestimate, and no one knows just how difficult it can be until you go through it yourself. Life isn't always easy, but you should be proud of yourself if you've taken the time to read this book. I'm extremely grateful that you've let me be a part of your life during this difficult time. I hope this book has been helpful to you and has given you not only direction, but also a sense of relief and the realization that you deserve the happiness you've always wanted.

ACKNOWLEDGMENTS

First and foremost, I'd like to thank my amazing parents, David and Dawne Young. Without them I would have not been able to experience so many of the things I have in life. They have always put my brother and me before themselves. They have been truly supportive of me during the entire process of creating this book. When I originally told them that I was in the process of creating a self-help book for others who are going through experiences similar to mine, it immediately brought tears to their eyes.

They have offered support throughout my divorce and they continually supported me through the rollercoaster of dating and relationships that I had during my journey to find love. They never made me feel guilty for bringing dates around, and they even encouraged it. They have always welcomed people that I have introduced to them and have only ever wanted happiness for me. Even though many of those people were not right for me, we still had a blast and a ton of fun adventures together. They are times I will never forget, and I thank you with all my heart.

I'd also like to thank my brother and sister-in-law, Bryce and Lucianna Young. My brother knows me better than anyone else on this planet. He has an instinct where he knows if someone is right for me or not within mere minutes. He also has no filter and will tell me the straight goods without sparing feelings. He's always looked out for me and my heart and, whether he knows it or not, he's still my overprotective older brother.

Lucianna is a beacon of support when it comes to my well-being. She would encourage me to enjoy my life no matter what stage I was at. She has countless phrases of wisdom that always take me by surprise. She has always been somewhat private with her life, but opens up to me in waves of humor and warmth. Her quirky sense of humor is what makes her so unique and enjoyable to be around.

I'd also like to thank my life. Whether we are all here for a reason or have a purpose in life, I believe that everything that happens to us is for a reason and it's how we deal with the events in our life that mold and create who we are as people. There were many times I looked negatively at my life, but I have become so grateful for the experiences that have happened to me. I have found that the negative experiences have been more of a development tool to me than the positive ones.

Without the negative experiences, I would have never written this book. It was my reactions to the negative experiences that created positive changes in my life. With every hurtful experience, I often found myself standing at a fork in the road with only two options: either let the experience overwhelm me, or do something about it and don't stop until I felt satisfied that I had changed something bad into something I could be thankful for.

Lastly, I'd like to thank my life-long friend, Leah Bolton, who's shown me over the past 21 years what true friendship is all about. She's always been there whenever I needed advice or someone to talk to or share a bottle of wine with. Much like myself, she has filled herself with knowledge from reading and participating in life events. She has always searched for the better in herself and used whatever life tools are available to her to continually grow her character, knowledge and well-being. She has inspired me never to give up on myself or love and has shown me understanding and patience throughout the course of it. Self-betterment is a privilege available to all of us if we choose to evaluate ourselves and have the courage to admit where our weaknesses are. Leah is the epiphany of what it takes to never give up on yourself, and she will never stop her self-growth.

Made in the USA
Thornton, CO
06/09/23 05:43:45

e3b1a6b6-c4bc-4ce8-9f21-9f0b6a53c127R01